PDCA
FOR ONGOING
SUCCESS

Increase efficiency, streamline processes, and enhance decision-making to drive continuous growth and sustainable success.

Author- MBB-Biswanath Subhash Panda

Website- https://mastermindcareerhub.com/mbb-biswanathspanda

Contact- connect@mbbbiswanathspanda.com

Book Description

PDCA for Ongoing Success:

Increase Efficiency, Streamline Processes, and Enhance Decision-Making to Drive Continuous Growth and Sustainable Success

Are you searching for a practical, proven framework to unlock your business's true potential? In *PDCA for Ongoing Success*, you'll discover how the Plan-Do-Check-Act (PDCA) methodology and the SMART PDCA-SDCA Cycle can revolutionize your approach to problem-solving, process improvement, and organizational growth. This book is not just a guide but a powerful toolkit that equips you with the strategies and tools to master continuous improvement in today's dynamic, competitive business environment.

This book offers a comprehensive roadmap for effectively implementing the PDCA cycle and its improved version, the SMART PDCA-SDCA Cycle, across teams, departments, and organizations, regardless of whether you are a business leader, manager, or team member. With real-world case studies from global giants like Toyota, Amazon, Starbucks, Intel, and Netflix, you'll gain invaluable insights into how this time-tested methodology can drive success across diverse industries, including manufacturing, e-commerce, hospitality, technology, and entertainment.

What You'll Learn:

- **Foundations of PDCA:** Understand the core principles behind the cycle and why it remains a cornerstone of continuous improvement.
- **SMART PDCA-SDCA Cycle:** Learn how this enhanced approach integrates continuous improvement (PDCA)

with process maintenance (SDCA) to ensure sustainable success.
- **Planning for Success:** Explore tools and techniques for identifying problems, setting SMART goals, and designing actionable plans.
- **Execution with Precision:** Learn how to implement strategies effectively, ensuring alignment with organizational objectives.
- **Performance Measurement:** Gain expertise in tracking progress, analyzing results, and refining processes for optimal efficiency.
- **Team Collaboration:** Discover strategies to foster alignment, define roles, and encourage teamwork to ensure seamless PDCA implementation.
- **Scaling and Sustainability:** Learn how to expand PDCA across departments and standardize processes to achieve long-term growth.

The Power of SMART PDCA-SDCA Cycle

This book introduces the SMART PDCA-SDCA Cycle, a hybrid approach to achieve measurable, sustainable improvement. The process combines the dynamic adaptability of PDCA with the stability of SDCA, emphasizing three essential prerequisites:

1. Being comfortable with discomfort during the cycles.
2. Valuing consistency over perfection.
3. Gaining the confidence of senior management for successful implementation.

This methodology ensures that organizations achieve and sustain progress through SMART goal-setting, targeted planning, and repeatable cycles of improvement and standardization.

Who Should Read This Book?

This book is essential for anyone passionate about driving change and achieving organizational excellence.

- Business leaders are seeking sustainable growth strategies.
- Managers are striving for better team collaboration and productivity.
- Professionals are eager to refine their problem-solving and decision-making skills.
- Students and researchers are exploring the practical applications of quality management methodologies.

Real-World Inspiration:
Delve into case studies that vividly illustrate the transformative power of the PDCA and the SMART PDCA-SDCA Cycle. These stories will inspire you and show you how to apply these methodologies to your organization, driving success and continuous improvement.

- Learn how Toyota redefined lean manufacturing by applying PDCA to reduce waste and improve production efficiency.
- Explore Amazon's approach to optimizing delivery systems and enhancing customer satisfaction through data-driven adjustments.
- Discover how Starbucks leveraged PDCA to boost employee engagement and service quality.
- Understand how Intel streamlined its product development cycle, reducing time-to-market and fostering innovation.
- See how Netflix continuously refines its recommendation algorithms and content delivery to delight its global user base.

Why This Book Stands Out:
Unlike purely theoretical texts, *PDCA for Ongoing Success* bridges the gap between strategy and execution. By incorporating the SMART PDCA-SDCA Cycle, this book shows how to sustain improvements and embed them in your organizational culture. Its unique selling points include practical insights, actionable

strategies, and real-world examples from global leaders, making it a comprehensive guide for continuous improvement. After reading this book, you'll feel informed, empowered, and ready to change your organization with the practical strategies you've gained.

By leveraging these methodologies, you'll be equipped to:

- Enhance decision-making processes with data-driven insights.
- Reduce inefficiencies and eliminate waste.
- Cultivate a culture of learning and adaptability.
- Strengthen customer satisfaction and employee engagement.
- Achieve measurable outcomes that align with strategic objectives.

Why Wait? Start Your Continuous Improvement Journey Today.
In today's fast-paced world, organizations that adapt and improve thrive. *PDCA for Ongoing Success* equips you with the practical tools, mindset, and strategies to build a resilient, high-performing organization. As soon as you finish reading, you'll feel ready to start your continuous improvement journey.

Whether you want to enhance small-scale operations or achieve large-scale success in your organization, PDCA for Ongoing Success will empower you to make meaningful, lasting changes. Each chapter provides actionable strategies and real-world examples, making the book applicable to various business scenarios. From problem-solving to scaling for growth, this book is your guide to continuous improvement.

Don't wait to start your continuous improvement journey. Order your copy of PDCA for Ongoing Success today and take the first step toward ongoing success!

Key Takeaway from this book:

1. "Transform your business with the ultimate guide to continuous improvement—PDCA for Ongoing Success is your blueprint for excellence."
2. "Discover the SMART PDCA-SDCA Cycle and unlock a sustainable approach to measurable progress and process mastery."
3. "From Toyota to Netflix, see how the PDCA cycle drives success—and learn how to apply it to your organization."
4. "Practical, insightful, and actionable—this book will change how you approach problem-solving, decision-making, and growth."

About the Author

Biswanath Subhash Panda, a Master Black Belt in Lean Six Sigma certified by the Indian Statistical Institute, Mumbai, and ASQ Certified Six Sigma Black Belt (CSSBB), brings over 30 years of profound expertise in process development and improvement. His significant impact on the manufacturing and service industries and his role as the co-founder of Mastermind Career Hub, a platform under the SBP SigmaL group, have empowered numerous working professionals through Lean Six Sigma certifications, boosting their career growth and professional recognition.

Throughout his illustrious career, Biswanath has served in key roles, including Head of Quality and R&D. He has successfully guided numerous Lean Six Sigma improvement projects, demonstrating his practical knowledge and expertise. His proficiency spans auto part development, IATF 16949 QMS implementation, and audits. As a lead auditor for ISO 9001, he upholds the highest quality and safety standards.

Biswanath, who holds a bachelor's degree in mechanical engineering, continues to inspire professionals with his mentorship and digital courses on Lean Six Sigma. His commitment to continuous learning and professional development is evident in his role as the co-founder of Mastermind Career Hub. He shares a fulfilling life with his wife, Sarada Panda, and is the proud father of two daughters, Sellora and Yellora.

Table of Contents

Book Description 2

About the Author 7

Chapter 1: Introduction...**10**

Understanding PDCA: A Story for Success 10

The Historical Context of PDCA 14

SMART PDCA-SDCA Cycle 22

Benefits of Implementing PDCA 29

PDCA in Action: Real-World Applications 32

Structure of This Book 40

Chapter 2: Planning for Problem-Solving................**45**

Identifying the Core Problem 47

Setting Measurable Goals for Improvement 49

Developing Actionable Steps 51

Allocating Resources and Responsibilities 53

Risk Assessment and Contingency Planning 56

Chapter 3: Executing with Precision...........................**58**

Implementing the Action Plan 58

Monitoring Progress in Real-Time 60

Ensuring Team Alignment and Accountability 62

Overcoming Obstacles During Execution 64

Maintaining Focus on Key Objectives 65

Chapter 4: Measuring Performance............................**67**

Defining Key Performance Indicators (KPIs) 67

Gathering Accurate Data for Analysis 69

Analyzing Results Against Goals 72

Identifying Gaps and Opportunities 74

Using Feedback for Continuous Improvement 76

Chapter 5: Learning and Adapting — 78
Analyzing What Worked and What Didn't 78

Adapting Strategies for Improvements 80

Integrating Feedback into Future Cycles 82

Fostering a Culture of Continuous Learning 83

Scaling Lessons Across the Organization 85

Chapter 6: Applying PDCA in Teams — 87
Building Team Alignment Around PDCA 87

Defining Roles and Responsibilities 89

Facilitating Collaboration for Problem-Solving 93

Tracking Progress and Accountability 96

Celebrating Wins and Learning Together 99

Chapter 7: Case Studies in PDCA — 101
Toyota: Revolutionizing Manufacturing with PDCA 101

Amazon: Enhancing Customer Satisfaction Through PDCA 106

Starbucks: Improving Employee Engagement Using PDCA 111

Intel: Streamlining Product Development with PDCA 116

Netflix: Continuously Enhancing User Experience with PDCA 122

Chapter 8: Scaling PDCA for Growth — 129
Expanding PDCA Across Departments 129

Standardizing Processes for Consistency 131

Leveraging Technology to Support PDCA 134

Training Teams for Scalable Implementation 138

Monitoring Long-Term Growth and Success 140

Book Summary of PDCA For Ongoing Success 144

A Heartfelt Request 148

Free Bonus- Audiobook 149

Chapter 1: Introduction

****

"Quality is not an act; it is a habit."

— **Aristotle**

What to expect in this chapter?

1. *An overview of the PDCA cycle with a success story.*
2. *A brief history of the PDCA method, its evolution in business practices, and the SMART PDCA-SDCA Cycle innovative technique.*
3. *Discover the SMART PDCA-SDCA Cycle and unlock a sustainable approach to measurable progress and process mastery.*
4. *Highlight the advantages of using the PDCA cycle in organizations for ongoing success.*
5. *Real-world application and Examples of how Indian businesses effectively apply PDCA to drive improvements and solve problems.*
6. *An outline of the book's chapters to learn from each section.*

Understanding PDCA: A Story for Success

In the late 1990s, the Pearl River School District in New York was a source of pride for its community. Parents sent their children there with high hopes for their future, and teachers worked tirelessly to shape young minds. Despite their dedication, however, the district began facing severe challenges. School test scores were falling, classrooms felt chaotic, and student engagement was in decline.

For the teachers and administrators, this was frustrating. They were doing their best, introducing new initiatives and strategies, but nothing seemed to stick. No consistency or structure was guiding their efforts. They tried everything they could think of, yet they couldn't figure out where they were going wrong. Meanwhile, parents lost trust in the system and worried about their children's future. *"What's happening to our district?"* they ask. *"How can we fix this?"*

The district's leadership understood they needed a solution, not just a band-aid. They couldn't keep reacting to problems as they appeared; they required a systematic way to improve. This was when they realized their core issue wasn't a lack of passion or ideas, but a lack of structure. They needed a framework to bring order and consistency to their efforts, guiding them in fixing problems and preventing them from arising.

That's when they discovered the PDCA (Plan-Do-Check-Act) cycle, also known as the Deming Cycle. PDCA provided a continual improvement process based on the scientific method: planning a change, implementing it, evaluating the results, and then acting on what was learned. Let's break it down: Planning involves identifying the problem and planning a change; Doing is about implementing the plan; Checking is evaluating the results; and Acting is making necessary adjustments based on the evaluation. It was straightforward but impactful, offering the district a structured approach to its problems.

The first phase of PDCA is *Planning,* and this began with the district asking tough questions: *What did they need? Where were their current systems failing, and how could they be improved?*

School leaders gathered data from various sources—test scores, teacher evaluations, student feedback, and parent concerns. As they delved into the information, the problems became more apparent. The curriculum lacked consistency across schools, and teachers weren't receiving the support needed to reach their goals. Student services were fragmented, leaving the most vulnerable children behind.

Armed with this input, the district crafted a strategic plan with clear goals for improvement. They focused on six key areas where the PDCA model could help: strategic planning, needs analysis, curriculum design and delivery, staff goal setting and evaluation, student services, and classroom instruction. With these priorities in place, they were ready to move on to the next phase.

The *Doing* phase was where the district put its plans into action. However, they didn't implement sweeping changes all at once. Instead, they worked methodically, step by step. For example, in curriculum design, they set up teams of teachers to review the existing curriculum, identify gaps, and recommend improvements. They didn't impose a new curriculum overnight but began with a pilot program in a few schools, monitoring how it performed in real classrooms.

The district introduced clear, consistent performance standards for teachers, but teachers still needed to realize what was expected. They were given goals aligned with the district's strategic plan and supported by professional development to help them achieve them. In classrooms, teachers focused on improving instruction by collaborating and gathering student feedback. PDCA allowed them to try innovative approaches while ensuring that they learned from their experiences.

Once these changes were underway, the district entered the *Checking* phase. The district's rigorous evaluation went beyond simply checking off boxes, striving to find actual results and measure the success of each initiative. They monitored student test scores, not just as ultimate outcomes but as tools for understanding deeper issues. Were the curriculum changes helping students grasp core concepts more effectively? Were teachers receiving enough support to meet their goals?

The results were encouraging but could have been better. Some schools showed marked improvements, while others continued to struggle. However, this didn't discourage the district. Instead, it reaffirmed their commitment to continual improvement. They didn't see setbacks as failures but as opportunities to gain experience and refine their approach.

In the *Acting* phase, the district solidified its commitment to long-term success. After analyzing the results from the checking phase, adjustments were made where needed. In schools where the new curriculum was working, it was expanded district-wide. In schools where teachers needed more support, training was increased, and additional resources were provided. It used data not to criticize, but to understand where it could improve.

Student services also saw improvements. By regularly reviewing student and parent feedback, the district tailored services more effectively to address each student's specific needs, particularly those who had been falling through the cracks.

As Pearl River School District fully embraced PDCA, the results became apparent. Test scores rose steadily, classrooms became more engaging, and teachers felt empowered to do their best work. Parents noticed these changes as their children began thriving in ways they hadn't seen before.

In 2001, the district's efforts were nationally recognized when it received the prestigious Malcolm Baldrige National Quality Award. This award celebrated its commitment to continual improvement and excellence in education. But for Pearl River, the award wasn't the goal—it was just a milestone in its **ongoing success**.

The district's story is a powerful example of how the PDCA cycle can lead to real, lasting change. By taking a systematic, thoughtful approach to improvement, they overcame their challenges and created a brighter future for their students, teachers, and the entire community. It's a reminder that success isn't a destination—it's a continuous journey. With PDCA as its guide, the Pearl River School District grew more robust with each improvement cycle.

The Historical Context of PDCA

In 1939, Dr Walter A. Shewhart integrated the scientific method with continuous improvement by organizing three key steps: *Specification, Production, and Inspection* in a straight line, as illustrated in "Fig. 1 Shewhart Cycle." He later suggests that these steps should follow a circular pattern rather than a straight line, reflecting the continuous nature of the mass production process. This approach involves forming a hypothesis, conducting experiments, and testing the results. Together, these three steps- Specification, Production, and Inspection—form a continuous improvement cycle.

Fig. 1- Shewhart Cycle 1939

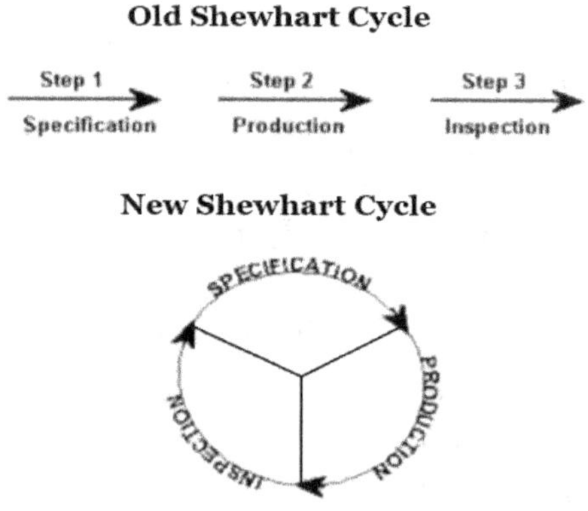

Old Shewhart Cycle

Step 1 → Specification   Step 2 → Production   Step 3 → Inspection

New Shewhart Cycle

Source- Adapted from Moen and Norman (2009)

In 1950, W. Edwards Deming modified Shewhart's cycle during an eight-day seminar on Statistical Quality Control (SQC) for managers and engineers at the Japanese Union of Scientists and Engineers (JUSE). Shewhart's three-step cycle-Specification, Production, Inspection- was transformed by Deming into a four-step process: *1. Design, 2. Produce, 3. Sell, and 4. Redesign through market research.* Prizing continuous interaction among design, production, sales, and redesign through market research in improving product quality and service. In Japan, this cycle became recognized as the "Deming Wheel." as shown in Fig. 2.

Fig. 2- Deming Wheel 1950

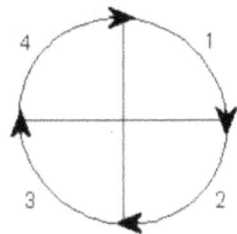

1. Design the product (with appropriate tests).
2. Make it; test it in the production line and in the laboratory.
3. Put it on the market.
4. Test it in service, through market research, find out what the user thinks of it, and why the non-user has not bought it.
5. *Re*-design the product, in the light of consumer reactions to quality and price.
Continue around and around the cycle.

Source- Adapted from Moen and Norman (2009)

Masaaki Imai's account of the Japanese executives' adaptation of the Deming Wheel from the 1950 JUSE seminar into the Plan-Do-Check-Act (PDCA) cycle in 1951, as depicted in "Fig. 3.1," is a significant milestone in the history of quality management. Imai's insights, shared in his 1986 book Kaizen: The Key to Japan's Competitive Success, underscore the evolution of the PDCA cycle. He draws a clear parallel between the Deming Wheel and the PDCA cycle, equating Design with Plan, Production with Do, Sales with Check, and Redesign through market research with Act.

The PDCA cycle is crucial in quality management. It is primarily focused on preventing error recurrence by setting and refining standards. Before the PDCA cycle can be effectively implemented, it is essential to stabilize the existing standards. This stabilization process is often called the SDCA (Standardize-Do-Check-Act) cycle, as shown in Fig. 3.2.

Question: What is the difference between PDCA and SDCA?

The PDCA cycle is used for process improvement, while the SDCA cycle plays a crucial role in preventing or maintaining the deterioration of processes that have already been improved. Once modifications are made, the SDCA cycle maintains and standardizes processes. This stabilization is a necessary step before moving on to further improvements through PDCA cycles.

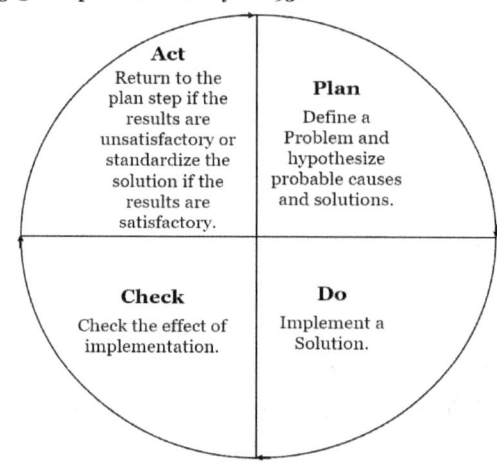

Fig. 3.1- Japanese PDCA Cycle 1951

Fig. 3.2- Standardize-Do-Check-Act (SDCA Cycle)

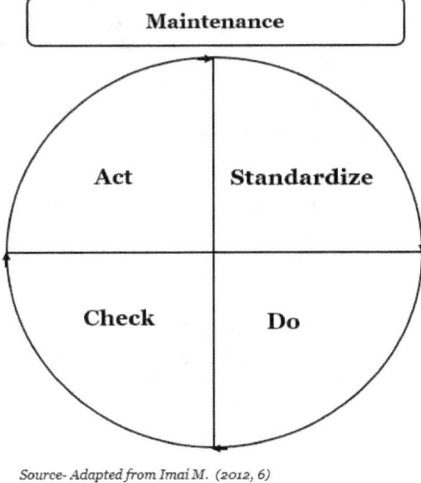

Source- Adapted from Imai M. (2012, 6)

The first PDCA cycle, developed to address shop-floor problems and prevent recurrence, is a robust model with many practical applications. Whether it's quality improvement, process enhancement, product design and development, service offerings, educational curricula, or healthcare, the PDCA cycle provides a comprehensive framework for understanding what needs to be done and the current position within the cycle.

Fig. 4- PDCA Cycle modified by Ishikawa 1985

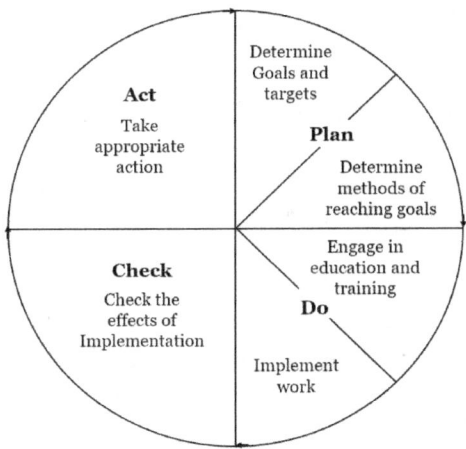

Source- Adapted from Moen and Norman (2010, 26)

In 1985, Kaoru Ishikawa modified the PDCA model by adding elements to the Plan and Do steps, as shown in "Fig. 4."

In his four-day seminars in 1980, Deming presented the PDSA version, arguing that the plan, do, check, and act version is inaccurate for Western audiences because the English word "check" means "to hold back."

In 1986, Deming reintroduced the Shewhart cycle, which came directly from the 1950 version (Deming Wheel), as shown in Fig. 5.

Fig. 5- Deming's PDSA Cycle 1986

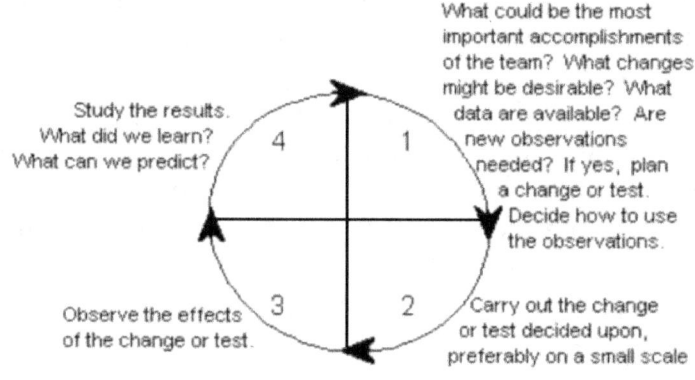

Step 5. Repeat Step 1, with knowledge accumulated.
Step 6. Repeat Step 2, and onward.

Source- Adapted from Moen and Norman (2009)

In 1993, Deming again modified the PDSA cycle and called it the Shewhart Cycle for Learning and Improvement of a Product or a Process—the PDSA cycle, as shown in Fig. 6.

Fig. 6- Deming's modified PDSA Cycle 1993

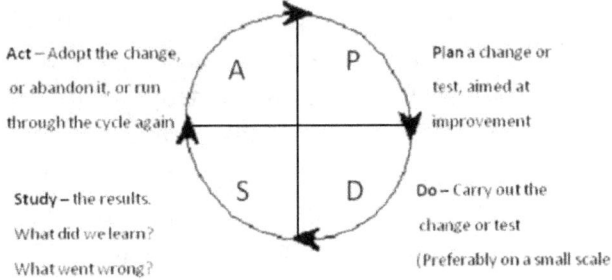

Source- Adapted from Moen and Norman (2009)

In 1994, Langley, Nolan, and Nolan refined the improvement cycle, renaming it the PDSA Cycle, as shown in "Fig. 7." The use of the word "study" in the third phase highlights the goal of this step: to build new knowledge. It does not confirm that a change led to improvement during a single test; it is also essential to predict whether the change will produce comparable results under varying conditions in the future. They introduced three fundamental questions to enhance the PDSA cycle:

1. What are we trying to accomplish?
2. How will we know that a change is an improvement?
3. What changes can we make that will lead to improvement?

Fig. 7- PDSA Cycle 1994

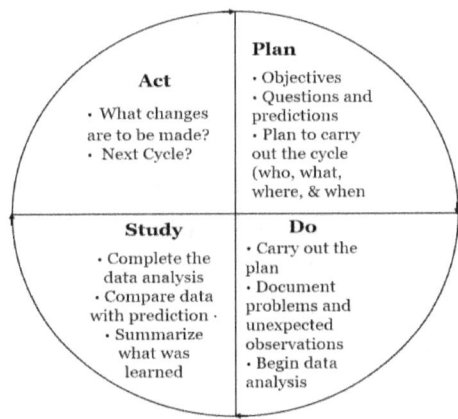

Source- Adapted from Moen and Norman (2010, 27)

Langley, Moen, Nolan, Nolan, Norman, and Provost combined the three fundamental questions with the PDSA cycle to create the API Model for Improvement foundation, as shown in "Fig. 8." These questions define the goal, measures, and potential changes. A set of seventy-two change concepts is provided to guide the use of the PDSA cycle for developing, testing, implementing, and spreading modifications that lead to improvement. This model can enhance organizational processes, products, and services, as well as personal endeavors. It aims to balance the motivation to take action with the value of thoughtful analysis before acting.

Fig. 8- Model for Improvement 1996

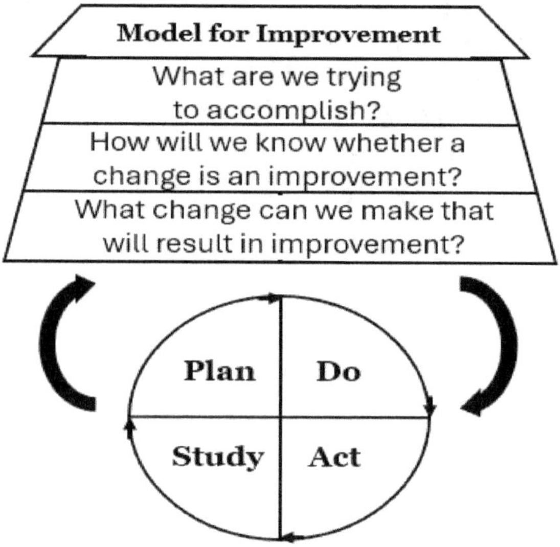

Source- Adapted from Moen and Norman (2010, 27)

As part of the ISO 9001 Quality Management System, the PDCA cycle is a versatile tool that can be applied to all organizational processes. Figure 9 demonstrates how ISO 9001 Clauses 4-10 align with the PDCA cycle, highlighting their adaptability and relevance across various contexts.

Fig. 9 PDCA APPROACH–ISO 9001:2015 QUALITY MANAGEMENT SYSTEM

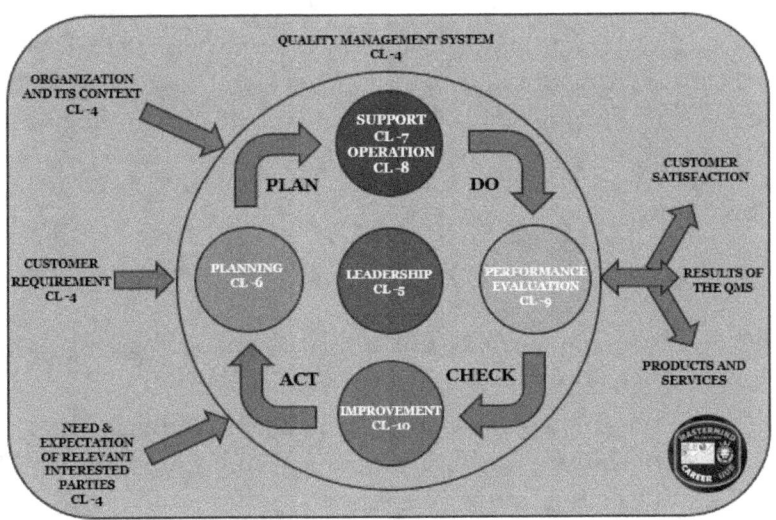

Source- ISO 9001:2015 Quality management systems — Requirements

The ISO PDCA cycle can be briefly described as follows:

Plan: establish the objectives of the system and its processes, identify the resources needed to deliver results in line with the customer's requirements and the organization's policies, and address risks and opportunities.

Do: implement what was planned.

Check: monitor and (where applicable) measure processes and the resulting products and services against policies, objectives, requirements, and planned activities, and report the results.

Act: take actions to improve performance, as necessary.

SMART PDCA-SDCA Cycle

The author recommends integrating the PDCA (Plan-Do-Check-Act) and SDCA (Standardize-Do-Check-Act) cycles to effectively achieve organizational goals. These cycles were implemented 3 to 4 times yearly for the best results.

To apply the SMART PDCA-SDCA Cycle, three essential prerequisites, known as the "3Cs," should be met:

1. *The* team should be *Comfortable with discomfort* during the SMART PDCA-SDCA cycle.
2. *Consistency* should be prioritized over perfection.
3. *Confidence* from senior management must be established as a critical support factor.

An example of the SMART PDCA-SDCA Cycle can be seen in a manufacturing or pharmaceutical company aiming to reduce internal quality PPM/DPMO by 50% from the current level of 1000 PPM/DPMO within one year.

- **S**pecific- Focused on reducing internal quality **PPM** (Parts Per Million)/DPMO (Defects Per Million Opportunities).
- **M**easurable- A targeted reduction of 50%.
- **A**chievable- This target is workable, as a 6-sigma process can achieve 3.4 PPM/DPMO.
- **R**ealistic- A 50% reduction is practical, though complete elimination is not.
- **T**ime-Bound—Set to be completed within one year.

SMART PDCA-SDCA Strategy- 3 or 4 cycles to achieve the objective.

Strategy 1: 3 SMART PDCA-SDCA cycles within one year, as shown in "Fig. 10".

- ❖ PDCA Cycle #1: 3 months
- ❖ SDCA Cycle #1: 1 month
- ❖ PDCA Cycle #2: 3 months
- ❖ SDCA Cycle #2: 1 month
- ❖ PDCA Cycle #3: 3 months
- ❖ SDCA Cycle #3: 1 month

Strategy 2–4 SMART PDCA-SDCA cycles within one year.

- ❖ PDCA Cycle #1: 2 months
- ❖ SDCA Cycle #1: 1 month
- ❖ PDCA Cycle #2: 2 months
- ❖ SDCA Cycle #2: 1 month
- ❖ PDCA Cycle #3: 2 months
- ❖ SDCA Cycle #3: 1 month
- ❖ PDCA Cycle #4: 2 months
- ❖ SDCA Cycle #4: 1 month

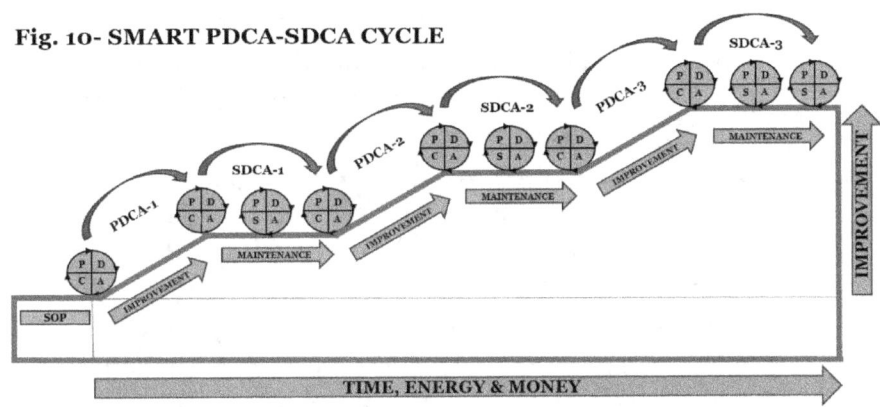

Fig. 10- SMART PDCA-SDCA CYCLE

HOW IS THE SMART PDCA-SDCA CYCLE IMPLEMENTED TO ACHIEVE ONGOING SUCCESS?

PDCA CYCLE 1-

Plan Phase:

The *Plan Phase,* the PDCA cycle's cornerstone, is where the problem is thoroughly analyzed, and a comprehensive strategy is meticulously crafted. This phase sets the direction for the entire cycle, making it a critical starting point for any improvement initiative.

1. **Define the Problem Relative to Ideal vs. Current:** The gap between the ideal quality level (zero defects) and the current state (1000 PPM) must be clearly defined. Internal defect reports, customer feedback, and production data are analyzed to understand the areas causing the most defects.
2. **Gemba Walk / Hypothesis Testing:** A Gemba walk observes processes on the shop floor and forms hypotheses about potential root causes, such as equipment calibration issues, operator errors, or material inconsistencies.
3. **Break Down the Problem Using the 80/20 Rule:** The Pareto principle applies to identify the 20% of defect types causing 80% of the internal PPM issues. This prioritization ensures that efforts are focused on areas with the greatest impact.
4. **Set SMART Goals and Targets:** A specific, measurable, achievable, realistic, and time-bound (SMART) goal will reduce internal quality PPM from 1000 to 500 within one year.
5. **Conduct Root Cause Analysis (RCA):** Tools like fishbone diagrams, 5 Why, or failure mode and effects analysis (FMEA) are used to uncover the underlying causes of defects.
6. **Develop an Implementation Plan:** A detailed plan addresses the identified root causes. Actions include upgrading equipment, refining operator training, and improving quality control checks.

7. **Create a Follow-Up Plan:** A follow-up plan is established to monitor the implementation's progress, assign responsibilities, and set review dates.
8. **Secure PDCA Approval from Management:** Senior management approval is sought to ensure alignment and support. Resources, budgets, and timelines are confirmed.

Do Phase:

In the *Do Phase,* the implementation plan is executed.

Implementation of the Plan: Actions are put into motion. For example:

- ➤ New equipment settings are calibrated.
- ➤ Revised training sessions are delivered to operators.
- ➤ Enhanced quality inspection protocols are deployed.
- ➤ Materials from alternate suppliers are tested.

The focus is on maintaining consistency and gathering data throughout the implementation process.

Check Phase:

The *Check Phase* verifies whether the implemented changes achieve the desired outcomes.

> *Verification of Results:* Quality control teams regularly measure PPM levels. Data is compared against baseline levels (1000 PPM) and the target (500 PPM). Any deviations are carefully analyzed to determine if adjustments are needed.

Act Phase:

The *Act Phase* focuses on institutionalizing the improvements and refining the processes.

> *Adapt, Adjust, and Update SOPs*: Standard operating procedures (SOPs) are updated to reflect the successful changes. Lessons learned are documented, and adjustments are made to ensure long-term sustainability.

SDCA Cycle-1: Standardizing and Maintaining Improvements

Once the initial PDCA cycle is completed, the SDCA (Standardize-Do-Check-Act) cycle is employed to sustain the improvements and integrate them into daily operations.

Standardize Phase:

> **Standardize the Improvement:** New best practices are standardized across the manufacturing process. Work instructions, quality inspection protocols, and operator manuals are updated to reflect the improvements.

Do Phase:

> **Maintain the Improved Process:** Regular audits and inspections are conducted to ensure compliance with the updated standards. Operators are continuously trained to reinforce the improved processes.

Check Phase:

> **Calculate Process Capability:** Statistical tools, such as process capability indices (Cp and Cpk), evaluate the consistency and stability of the improved processes.

Act Phase:

>**Take Action to Improve Process Capability:**
>Further adjustments are made if the process capability falls short of expectations. Continuous monitoring ensures that any deviations are promptly addressed.

Repeating the PDCA-SDCA Cycles for Sustained Growth

The PDCA-SDCA cycles are repeated three to four times a year. Each cycle builds upon the previous one, ensuring continuous improvement and sustained growth.

1. In the **second cycle**, additional root causes are addressed, focusing on secondary contributors to defects.
2. The **third cycle** may concentrate on cross-departmental collaboration to tackle systemic issues.
3. By the **fourth cycle**, the organization transitions into a culture of continuous improvement, where proactive problem-solving becomes embedded in daily operations.

Practical Implementation: A Case in Manufacturing

A mid-sized automotive parts manufacturing company followed this roadmap to reduce internal quality PPM from 1000 to 500.

Cycle 1: Tackling Major Defects

During the first cycle, a Gemba walk revealed that misalignment in the assembly equipment accounted for 60% of the defects. Immediate actions included recalibrating the machinery and retraining operators. Within three months, PPM was reduced by 20%.

Cycle 2: Enhancing Quality Inspections

The second cycle focused on strengthening the quality control system. Advanced inspection tools were introduced, and defective trends were analyzed in real time. Another 15% reduction in PPM was achieved.

Cycle 3: Optimizing Material Supply

In the third cycle, material inconsistencies were identified as a significant issue. Collaboration with suppliers led to stricter material quality standards. This resulted in a further 10% reduction.

Cycle 4: Institutionalizing Improvements

In the last cycle, all improvements were standardized through updated SOPs and frequent audits. The internal PPM reached the 500 target, completing the one-year goal.

Conclusion

The SMART PDCA-SDCA cycle is a structured and adaptive framework designed to drive continuous improvement and sustain success across processes. By integrating the principles of problem-solving and standardization, this cycle ensures organizations can achieve both short-term goals and long-term growth. Its implementation is systematic, balancing meticulous planning, effective execution, and rigorous standardization.

The process begins with the **SMART PDCA cycle**, in which clear, actionable objectives are set using the SMART criteria: Specific, Measurable, Achievable, Realistic, and Time-bound. During the **Plan phase**, problems are defined, root causes are analyzed, and actionable solutions are designed. The **Do phase** ensures these solutions are implemented in a controlled manner. Progress is monitored during the Check phase, with outcomes verified against the objectives. Finally, successful improvements are institutionalized in the Act phase, and any necessary adjustments are made to refine the process further.

Once improvements are implemented, the **SDCA cycle** is employed to sustain these gains. This phase focuses on standardizing the improved practices to ensure consistency and reliability. Processes are regularly monitored to maintain efficiency, and further opportunities for refinement are identified. This iterative approach fosters a culture of continual learning and adaptation, enabling teams to align their efforts with organizational goals.

The true strength of the SMART PDCA-SDCA cycle lies in its adaptability. It can apply to diverse industries and processes, from manufacturing to service delivery. By focusing on systematic improvements and embracing a culture of accountability and innovation, this methodology enables organizations to navigate challenges, seize opportunities, and achieve sustained success in an ever-changing environment.

Benefits of Implementing PDCA

Some key benefits make PDCA a valuable approach for driving ongoing success.

1. Promotes Continuous Improvement:

PDCA encourages a culture of ongoing evaluation and refinement, ensuring processes continually improve.

Continuous improvement leads to higher efficiency, reduced waste, and better performance, keeping organizations competitive in a changing market.

2. Simplifies Problem-Solving:

PDCA breaks problems into smaller, manageable steps, making it easier to identify the root cause and develop solutions.

This structured approach leads to quicker resolutions and minimizes disruptions in business operations.

3. Enhances Decision-Making:

PDCA helps teams make more informed, strategic decisions by using data and analysis at every stage.

Better decision-making reduces risks, improves accuracy, and leads to more effective actions that positively impact business outcomes.

4. Encourages Employee Engagement:

The cycle involves team members in each phase, empowering them to contribute ideas and take ownership of the process.

Engaged employees are more motivated, productive, and innovative, strengthening the organization's success.

5. Applicable to All Industries:

PDCA demonstrates its adaptability by seamlessly integrating across sectors such as manufacturing, healthcare, IT, and services.

Its application ensures that organizations of any size and type can benefit from its principles to achieve their specific goals.

6. Reduces Costs and Wastage:

The PDCA iterative process identifies inefficiencies and operational waste.

Reducing waste and optimizing processes lowers operational costs, leading to better resource management and increased profits.

7. Build a Culture of Accountability:

PDCA holds individuals and teams accountable for the outcomes of their actions, promoting a sense of responsibility.

Accountability fosters a results-driven culture where everyone strives to achieve the best possible outcomes.

8. Drives Innovation and Adaptability:

The Act phase of PDCA encourages reflection and learning, leading to innovative ideas and creative solutions.

In today's challenging environment, quickly adapting and innovating is crucial for staying ahead of competitors.

9. Supports Long-Term Success:

PDCA focuses on sustainable growth and improvement by continuously refining strategies and processes.

Organizations that use PDCA are more likely to achieve consistent progress and long-term success than to experience temporary gains.

10. Facilitates Better Communication:

PDCA promotes clear communication and collaboration among team members, ensuring everyone is aligned with objectives and progress.

Better communication leads to more efficient teamwork and helps avoid misunderstandings that can derail projects.

Implementing the PDCA cycle in organizations offers many benefits beyond problem-solving. It fosters a culture of continuous improvement, empowers employees, drives innovation, and promotes sustainable growth. By adopting

PDCA, businesses can streamline operations, make data-driven decisions, and stay competitive in an ever-strengthened landscape.

PDCA in Action: Real-World Applications

The PDCA (Plan-Do-Check-Act) cycle is a versatile tool that can be applied to various industries and scenarios. Its structured approach to problem-solving and continuous improvement makes it a popular choice for businesses aiming to enhance their processes, reduce waste, and boost efficiency. Here are a few real-world examples of how organizations successfully implement PDCA.

1. Manufacturing Quality Control

- *Plan:* A manufacturing company identifies a recurring issue with defective products on its assembly line.
- *Do:* They introduce a new quality control process at specific checkpoints.
- *Check:* The team monitors the defect rate and finds a 30% reduction in faulty products.
- *Act:* The new quality control process is adopted across all production lines following positive results.

Outcome: Improved product quality and a significant decrease in production waste.

2. Customer Service Improvement

- *Plan:* A retail company receives customer feedback about long wait times in its service centers.
- *Do:* They train staff on faster customer interaction techniques.
- *Check:* The average customer service time is reviewed and shows a 40% improvement.

> *Act:* The training program is rolled out company-wide to standardize quick and efficient service.

Outcome: Enhanced customer satisfaction and reduced wait times.

3. Software Development Process

> *Plan:* A software team identifies delays in their release schedule due to inefficient bug tracking.
> *Do:* They implement a new bug-tracking tool to streamline the reporting process.
> *Check:* The tool's effectiveness is evaluated, demonstrating faster resolution of software issues.
> *Act:* The tool becomes a standard part of the team's development workflow.

Outcome: Increased efficiency in handling bugs and faster software releases.

4. Healthcare Patient Care Improvement

> *Plan:* A hospital notices increased patient wait times in the emergency department.
> *Do:* They pilot a triage system to prioritize patients based on severity.
> *Check:* Data from the pilot shows a 50% reduction in wait times for critical cases.
> *Act:* The triage system is implemented across all emergency departments.

Outcome: Improved patient care and faster response times in emergencies.

5. Supply Chain Optimization

> *Plan:* A logistics company identifies inefficiencies in its supply chain management.

- ➢ *Do:* They introduce a real-time tracking system for shipments.
- ➢ *Check:* Analysis reveals a 25% improvement in delivery times.
- ➢ *Act:* The tracking system is adopted for all operations to enhance supply chain visibility.

Outcome: More reliable deliveries and higher customer satisfaction.

6. Energy Conservation in Facilities Management

- ➢ *Plan:* A facility manager aims to reduce the energy consumption of a commercial building.
- ➢ *Do:* They test energy-efficient lighting systems in one building section.
- ➢ *Check:* Energy usage data is reviewed, showing a 20% reduction.
- ➢ *Act:* Energy-efficient lighting is installed throughout the facility.

Outcome: Lower energy bills and a smaller environmental footprint.

7. Marketing Campaign Optimization

- ➢ *Plan:* A company's recent marketing campaign did not generate the expected engagement.
- ➢ *Do:* They redesign the campaign content based on audience feedback.
- ➢ *Check:* The engagement metrics have been analyzed, revealing a 35% increase in responses.
- ➢ *Act:* The improved strategy applies to future marketing efforts.

Outcome: Higher engagement and better-targeted marketing campaigns.

8. Inventory Management in Retail

- ➤ *Plan:* A retail store faces frequent stockouts and overstock.
- ➤ *Do:* They implement a new inventory tracking software for better demand forecasting.
- ➤ *Check:* The store's stock levels are reviewed, showing reduced stock-outs and excess inventory.
- ➤ *Act:* The software is integrated into all store locations.

Outcome: Optimized inventory levels and increased sales because of better product availability.

9. Project Management in Construction

- ➤ *Plan:* A construction company experiences project delays because of poor time management.
- ➤ *Do:* They introduce a project management tool to track timelines and deadlines.
- ➤ *Check:* The tool's impact is measured, showing a 15% increase in on-time project completions.
- ➤ *Act:* The project management tool becomes standard across all construction projects.

Outcome: Improved project timelines and enhanced team coordination.

10. Reducing Food Waste in Restaurants

- ➤ *Plan:* The restaurant chain identifies significant food waste during peak hours.
- ➤ *Do:* They introduce portion control techniques and a new ordering system.
- ➤ *Check:* Waste levels are analyzed and show a 30% reduction in food waste.
- ➤ *Act:* The changes are adopted across all branches of the restaurant chain.

Outcome: Lower food waste and increased profitability through cost savings.

Several Indian companies have successfully implemented the PDCA (Plan-Do-Check-Act) cycle to improve processes, enhance productivity, and ensure continuous improvement. Here are a few examples:

1. Tata Steel:

Tata Steel, one of India's largest steel manufacturers, has long advocated adopting quality management systems. It adopted the PDCA cycle to improve its manufacturing processes and customer satisfaction.

- *Plan:* The company analyzed the root cause to identify inefficiencies in its manufacturing process and product quality issues.
- *Do:* Tata Steel implemented new quality control mechanisms on the shop floor, ensuring workers followed standard operating procedures.
- *Check:* They monitored performance metrics, including defect rates and operational efficiency, and compared them against predetermined targets.
- *Act:* Based on the results, Tata Steel made further improvements, training employees in problem-solving techniques and refining processes that needed more attention.

This PDCA application helped Tata Steel reduce waste, improve product quality, and enhance customer satisfaction. It also contributed to the company receiving the prestigious Deming Prize for quality in 2008.

2. Maruti Suzuki:

Maruti Suzuki, India's leading automobile manufacturer, implemented the PDCA cycle to streamline production processes, reduce defects, and improve vehicle quality.

- *Plan:* Maruti Suzuki identified inefficiencies in its assembly line that led to defects in the final products.
- *Do:* The company introduced specific measures, such as improving the supply chain and re-engineering production processes.
- *Check:* Maruti regularly tracked vehicle quality through in-line checks and quality inspections.
- *Act:* Based on feedback from the check phase, Maruti implemented continuous training for its workers and upgraded its equipment to prevent future defects.

Implementing PDCA enabled Maruti Suzuki to improve product quality, reduce lead times, and improve customer satisfaction.

3. Mahindra & Mahindra:

Mahindra & Mahindra, a prominent Indian automotive and tractor manufacturer, integrated PDCA into its production and supply chain management processes.

- *Plan:* The company analyzed supply chain delays affecting production timelines.
- *Do:* They restructured their procurement process, implemented vendor performance metrics, and introduced new logistics solutions.
- *They measured the impact of these changes by tracking key performance indicators, including* procurement time, inventory levels, and production output.
- *Act:* Based on the findings, Mahindra took corrective actions, such as renegotiating vendor contracts and implementing lean inventory practices.

This PDCA implementation helped Mahindra streamline its supply chain, reduce costs, and maintain timely delivery schedules, contributing to its robust business growth.

4. Wipro:

Wipro, one of India's largest IT and consulting firms, adopted PDCA in its quality management and software development processes.

- *Plan:* The company identified gaps in deliverable quality and service timelines.
- *Do:* Wipro introduced standard operating procedures (SOPs) for coding practices, project management, and client communications.
- *Check:* They performed regular audits and reviews of project deliverables, measuring them against established quality standards and timelines.
- Act: Based on the audits, they took corrective actions, including revising SOPs, providing training to teams, and realigning resources.

By using PDCA, Wipro achieved higher customer satisfaction, reduced project delays, and improved the overall quality of its services.

5. Reliance Industries:

Reliance Industries, a significant player in oil, petrochemicals, and retail, implemented the PDCA cycle to optimize operational efficiency across its refineries and retail chains.

- *Plan:* Reliance focused on reducing operational costs and improving the efficiency of its refining processes.
- *Do:* They made operational changes, such as introducing modern technologies and improving energy management systems.

> *Check:* The company closely monitored key performance indicators, such as energy consumption, production output, and operational downtime.
> *Act:* Based on the findings, Reliance fine-tuned its processes, introduced new maintenance schedules, and trained employees on energy conservation techniques.

The PDCA approach helped Reliance Industries significantly improve energy efficiency and operational performance, reducing costs while enhancing productivity.

6. *Godrej Consumer Products*:

Godrej Consumer Products applied the PDCA method in its supply chain and production planning to ensure high-quality consumer goods.

> *Plan:* Godrej identified inefficiencies in its production line that were causing delays and affecting product quality.
> *Do:* The company implemented new inventory management and quality control processes, ensuring a smoother workflow.
> *Check:* Regular audits and quality checks were conducted to ensure the changes had the desired effect.
> *Act:* Based on the findings, Godrej made further adjustments, improving supplier management and introducing worker training programs.

The result was improved product consistency, reduced lead times, and better overall performance.

These examples illustrate how the PDCA cycle can be applied to various industries to address specific challenges. From improving product quality in manufacturing to optimizing customer service and PDCA implementation across Indian companies, they highlight the method's versatility across industries. Whether in manufacturing, IT services, or consumer goods, PDCA has proven to be a practical framework for driving continuous improvement, reducing waste, and enhancing product and service quality.

Structure of This Book

In Chapter 2, we can learn effective ways to identify and prioritize issues.

1. How do we uncover the root cause of issues and define the problem clearly?
2. Creating specific, achievable targets that guide the problem-solving process.
3. Breaking down solutions into straightforward, manageable tasks for effective implementation.
4. Ensuring teams, tools, and timelines are aligned for smooth execution.
5. Identifying potential obstacles and preparing backup plans for successful outcomes.

In Chapter 3, we can learn about Ensuring the successful implementation of plans-

1. Step-by-step guidance on putting the plan into action effectively.
2. How do you track tasks and performance throughout the execution phase?
3. Keeping everyone focused and accountable to ensure smooth execution.
4. Strategies for identifying and handling challenges that arise in real-time.
5. Staying committed to the primary goals and avoiding distractions.

In Chapter 4, we can learn how to check and analyze outcomes.

1. How do you choose the right metrics to track progress and success?
2. Techniques for collecting reliable data to measure outcomes.
3. Comparing actual performance with planned objectives to assess effectiveness.
4. Recognizing areas for improvement and refining future actions.
5. Leveraging performance data to inform the next PDCA cycle and drive ongoing growth.

In Chapter 5, we can learn how to close the feedback loop for continuous improvement.

1. Reviewing successes and failures to extract valuable lessons.
2. How to adjust plans based on insights from the current PDCA cycle.
3. Using feedback to refine processes and enhance future performance.
4. Encouraging teams to embrace learning and adapt to change.
5. Applying learned insights across teams and departments for broader impact.

In Chapter 6, we can learn how to create a collaborative environment for process refinement.

1. Ensuring everyone understands and supports the PDCA approach.
2. Clarifying team roles to ensure smooth execution of the PDCA cycle.
3. Encouraging open communication and teamwork to solve issues effectively.

4. How do we monitor team activities and ensure accountability during PDCA cycles?
5. Recognizing achievements and sharing lessons to improve future team efforts.

In Chapter 7, we can learn some real-world examples of businesses thriving with "**PDCA for Ongoing Success**.

1. How does Toyota use the "*PDCA for Ongoing Success*" to improve production efficiency and reduce waste, becoming a leader in lean manufacturing?
2. How Amazon applied the "*PDCA for Ongoing Success*" to improve delivery speed, optimize inventory management, and enhance customer experience.
3. How Starbucks implemented "*PDCA for Ongoing Success*" to refine employee training programs, resulting in higher engagement, improved service quality, and increased customer satisfaction.
4. How Intel applied the "*PDCA for Ongoing Success*" to optimize product development processes, reducing time-to-market and increasing innovation efficiency.
5. How Netflix used "*PDCA for Ongoing Success*" to fine-tune its recommendation algorithm and content delivery, ensuring continuous user satisfaction and engagement improvement.

In Chapter 8, we can learn about expanding small-scale improvements across the organization.

1. How do we apply the PDCA cycle beyond individual teams to the entire organization?
2. Creating standardized procedures to ensure PDCA is consistently applied at scale.
3. Using digital tools and software to automate, track, and optimize PDCA activities.
4. Ensuring employees at all levels understand and can apply PDCA effectively.

5. How do we measure the impact of PDCA over time and adjust for sustained growth?

3 Questions-

Q1. How does the PDCA framework drive continuous business success?

A. The PDCA framework (Plan-Do-Check-Act) fosters continuous success by encouraging organizations to make small, incremental improvements that build. Businesses can consistently enhance efficiency and productivity by planning, implementing, evaluating, and adjusting processes, leading to long-term success.

Q2. What are the key steps of PDCA, and why are each crucial for problem-solving?

A. The four key steps of PDCA are:

- *Plan*: Identify the problem and design a solution. This step is crucial for laying a solid foundation for improvements.
- *Do*: Implement the solution on a small scale to test its effectiveness.
- *Check*: Analyze the results to see if the solution works.
- *Act*: If successful, implement the solution thoroughly. If not, make adjustments and repeat the cycle.

Q3. How can adopting PDCA improve daily operations and decision-making in modern businesses?

A. Adopting PDCA improves daily operations by creating a structured, repeatable process for continuous improvement. It empowers teams to tackle problems systematically, test solutions, and make data-driven decisions, leading to more efficient processes and better outcomes.

Summary of Chapter 1: *Introduction*

In this chapter, readers are introduced to the foundations of PDCA, including its history, principles, and core benefits. PDCA originated as a method to enhance quality and problem-solving in manufacturing, but it has since evolved into a versatile framework across industries and organizational functions. The cycle starts with the *Plan* phase, where objectives are set, potential solutions are explored, and a roadmap for action is created. The *Do* phase involves executing the plan and observing the results. In the *Check* phase, data is analyzed to assess whether the objectives were met. In the Act phase, adjustments are made to refine processes and prepare for the next cycle.

Chapter 2: Planning for Problem-Solving

****

"It is not enough to do your best; you must know what to do and then do your best."

— W. Edwards Deming

Story Planning for Problem-Solving: *The HCA FOCUS PDCA*

- *Find* a process to improve.
- *Organize* a team that understands the process.
- *Clarify* current knowledge of the process.
- *Understand* the causes of variation.
- *Select* the improvement strategy.

In the early 1990s, the Hospital Corporation of America (HCA) faced significant challenges in managing patient care effectively across its extensive network of hospitals. With rising operational costs, an increasing patient volume, and the growing need for efficiency, the leadership realized that an innovative approach was essential to improving patient outcomes and operational efficiency. That's when HCA implemented the FOCUS PDCA method, a continuous improvement process designed to optimize healthcare services.

The "FOCUS" part of the process identifies areas that need improvement. The PDCA cycle then takes over to drive the changes. HCA applied the FOCUS PDCA model in a specific area—emergency room (ER) operations, which were often the busiest and most chaotic sections of the hospitals. Delays in patient care and long wait times frustrated patients, which affected both the quality of care and patient satisfaction.

Planning, essential to HCA's initiative's success, was the first phase of the PDCA cycle. The leadership team at HCA began by thoroughly analyzing their ER operations to understand the root causes of the problems. They recognized that the main issue was the triage bottleneck, where patients were evaluated and assigned priority levels based on the severity of their conditions. This time-consuming process often led to delays in admitting patients for further treatment.

The planning phase began with gathering data to improve triage efficiency. HCA's team examined the time to triage a patient, the factors that slow the process, and the impact on overall patient flow. They also reviewed historical data on patient wait times, patient volume at various times of day, and the impact of staffing levels on operations. This comprehensive data collection was essential to making informed decisions about proceeding.

After compiling the data, the next phase of the planning process was to lay out specific objectives. HCA aimed to reduce patient wait times by 20% within the next quarter. They knew that achieving this required a detailed plan that addressed triage, staff training, equipment availability, and workflow optimization. They aim to streamline the triage process by implementing standardized protocols and empowering triage nurses to make quicker decisions.

With clear goals in place, HCA's leadership mapped *out its strategy.* The plan was to redesign the triage process to achieve faster assessment times. They introduced a new system that diverted low-risk patients who didn't require immediate attention to a fast-track lane. This freed up time and resources for more critical cases. They ensured that equipment such as blood pressure monitors and EKG machines was readily available, minimizing delays caused by resource shortages.

The final part of the planning phase was ensuring the staff were fully trained and prepared for the changes. HCA held workshops for its ER teams, during which nurses and doctors were trained on the new protocols and how to use the fast-track lane effectively. They also emphasized the importance of teamwork and communication in reducing delays and improving the patient experience.

By the end of the planning phase, HCA had a comprehensive, data-driven plan to address the issues it faced in the ER. This structured approach ensured everyone understood the objectives, the steps needed to achieve them, and the expected outcomes. The planning phase sets the foundation for successfully executing PDCA's "Do" phase, where these changes will be implemented.

Through the FOCUS PDCA model, HCA significantly improved its ER operations, ultimately reducing wait times and increasing patient satisfaction. The success of the planning phase demonstrated the PDCA cycle's power in healthcare settings, highlighting how a well-thought-out plan can lead to meaningful, sustainable improvements.

Identifying the Core Problem

Root cause analysis (RCA) is the ultimate weapon for identifying chronic problems. The six essential RCA tools are presented in a chronological order to achieve effectiveness and ongoing success.

1. **Gemba Walk**: Start with a Gemba walk to observe the actual process and understand where issues occur. This firsthand observation helps identify potential problems.
2. **Brainstorming**: After gathering initial insights from the Gemba walk, engage stakeholders in brainstorming sessions to generate ideas about the potential causes of the problems observed.
3. **Fishbone Diagram (Cause & effect diagram)**: Use this diagram to categorize and visualize the potential

causes generated during brainstorming. It helps identify root causes by breaking them down into 4M/ 6M categories {**Manpower, Material, Method, Machine**, Measurement, and Mother Nature (Environment)} in manufacturing or 6P categories (Policy, People, Process, Product, Place, and Promotion) in service.
4. **5 Why Analysis**: Once potential causes are identified using the Fishbone Diagram, apply the 5 Whys or Why-Why analysis technique to delve deeper into each identified cause. Ask "why" 5 times or repeatedly until the root cause is identified.
5. **Flowchart**: Create a flowchart of the process to visualize the steps involved. This tool helps pinpoint workflow breakdowns or inefficiencies.
6. **Pareto Analysis**: Use this analysis to prioritize the identified root causes based on their impact. You can address the most significant issues by focusing on the "vital few" causes (the top 20%).

3 Advanced RCA Tools-

1. **FMEA (Failure Mode and Effects Analysis)**: After identifying the fundamental causes, conduct FMEA to evaluate the potential failure modes associated with each cause, assessing their severity, occurrence, and detection.
2. **8D Analysis**: Apply the 8D method to implement corrective actions and ensure effective and sustainable solutions. This structured approach emphasizes teamwork and problem-solving.
3. **DMAIC (Define, Measure, Analyze, Improve, Control)**: "If the root cause and the solution are unknown, DMAIC is recommended. While DMAIC is associated with Six Sigma projects, it can be integrated at the end of the RCA process to ensure that improvements are effectively implemented, measured, and sustained.

This chronological order allows for a systematic approach to problem identification and resolution, ensuring thorough analysis and effective action planning.

Setting Measurable Goals for Improvement

In the planning phase of the PDCA cycle, setting measurable goals is crucial for guiding the problem-solving process. With clear targets, assessing progress and determining whether improvements have been achieved becomes easier. To achieve the best results, goals should be clear and realistic, and specific actions should be taken to address the problem, ensuring they are channeled effectively.

Measurable goals provide a roadmap for improvement, helping teams stay on track and make necessary adjustments. To do this, each goal must be defined with quantifiable metrics. The process begins with understanding the problem, identifying the desired outcomes, and determining how success will be measured. This approach helps clarify what needs to be achieved and establishes a foundation for ongoing improvement.

The Importance of Measurable Goals in PDCA

Measurable goals are vital for several reasons. First, they offer clarity. Without clear and measurable goals, it is easy to lose direction during problem-solving. Specific targets help teams break complex problems into manageable actions, making it easier to track progress. Second, measurable goals enable accountability. When goals are well-defined, assessing whether they have been met becomes easier, helping individuals and teams to be held accountable for their performance. Lastly, measurable goals ensure continuous improvement. By tracking and measuring progress, teams can identify what works and what doesn't, leading to adjustments that foster long-term success.

Three Goal-Setting Tools

1. SMART Goals
SMART goals, which are specific, measurable, achievable, relevant, and time-bound, are used for setting clear and actionable objectives. This method ensures that goals are defined in a way that makes it easier to evaluate success. Each aspect of SMART goals helps refine the target's focus and clarity. For instance, a vague goal like "improve customer satisfaction" can be turned into a SMART goal by specifying, "Increase customer satisfaction by 15% within the next six months, based on quarterly survey results."

2. OKRs (Objectives and Key Results)
Objectives and Key Results (OKRs) are another popular tool for setting measurable goals. This approach defines broad objectives and breaks them into specific, measurable key results. The objective provides direction, while the key results ensure that progress toward the objective is quantifiable. For example, an objective might be to "improve product quality," and the key results could include "reducing defect rates by 50% in the next quarter" or "increasing customer retention by 25%."

3. Balanced Scorecard
The Balanced Scorecard is a strategic tool for setting goals across an organization's different areas. It helps create a balanced view of success by setting goals not only in terms of financial performance but also from the customer, internal process, and learning perspectives. This tool ensures improvements are targeted across multiple organizational dimensions, leading to comprehensive growth.

A Tool to Measure Progress: Key Performance Indicators (KPIs)

Key Performance Indicators (KPIs) are critical for measuring progress toward goals. KPIs provide specific metrics that allow teams to assess how well they are performing against their goals. By regularly monitoring KPIs, teams can determine if their strategies are working and whether they are on track to achieve the desired outcomes. For example, if the goal is to reduce customer complaints, the KPI might be the "number of complaints received monthly." If the goal is to increase production efficiency, the KPI could be "units produced per hour."

Developing Actionable Steps

In the PDCA cycle, after identifying and prioritizing problems and setting measurable goals, the next critical step in the planning phase is developing actionable steps. Solutions must be broken down into manageable tasks that are clear, achievable, and practical for effective implementation. This organizes the problem-solving process, enabling teams to implement improvements more successfully.

Developing actionable steps ensures that the solution does not remain abstract or theoretical. Instead, it is transformed into specific actions that can be executed precisely. This approach makes tracking progress easier, allows adjustments when necessary, and helps achieve the desired results.

Why Actionable Steps Are Important

Actionable steps serve as the bridge between the planning and execution stages of the PDCA cycle. Without precise tasks, even the most well-planned solutions can falter during implementation. When significant problems are broken down into smaller, manageable tasks, it becomes easier for team members to understand what needs to be done and how to do it.

Potential obstacles can also be identified early by breaking solutions into specific tasks. For example, planning for this in advance can prevent delays if one task depends on completing another. This systematic approach ensures the project stays on schedule and that resources are used efficiently.

Steps to Create Actionable Tasks

1. Clarify the Solution
The first step in developing actionable tasks is ensuring the solution is clearly understood. If the solution to a problem is ambiguous, it won't be easy to translate it into specific actions. Therefore, it is essential to define the solution precisely. For example, if the goal is to improve customer satisfaction, the solution might involve streamlining the customer service process, reducing response times, or improving communication channels. Once the solution is clarified, breaking it down into smaller steps becomes more accessible.

2. Break Down the Solution into Smaller Tasks
After clarifying the solution, break it down into smaller, actionable tasks. Each task should represent a specific action that contributes to implementing the solution. For instance, if the solution involves streamlining a process, one task could be "conducting a process review," while another could be "training employees on new procedures." Breaking the solution into smaller tasks makes the project more manageable, and each step can be monitored and evaluated individually.

3. Prioritize and Sequence Tasks
Once the tasks have been identified, they should be prioritized and sequenced logically. Some tasks may need to be completed before others can begin, while some may have a more significant impact on the overall success of the solution. Determining the order in which tasks should be completed makes the implementation process smoother, reducing the chances of delays or inefficiencies.

4. Assign Responsibilities
For actionable steps to be practical, responsibilities must be

assigned to specific individuals or teams. Each task should have a clear owner who is accountable for its completion. This creates a sense of responsibility and ensures that no task is overlooked. Assigning clear roles helps distribute the workload evenly so that no individual or team is overburdened.

5. Set Deadlines and Milestones

Each task should include a deadline. Setting deadlines ensures that the project progresses promptly and tasks are completed within a reasonable time limit. Besides deadlines, setting milestones can help track progress at various stages of the project. Milestones serve as checkpoints to review progress, make adjustments as needed, and keep the team focused on achieving the overall goal.

Monitoring and Adjusting Actionable Steps

Even after actionable steps are developed and implemented, continuous monitoring is necessary to ensure that progress is being made as planned. If tasks are not yielding the expected results, adjustments may be required. Sometimes, tasks must be redefined, reordered, or assigned to different individuals. Flexibility is essential in this process, allowing the team to adapt to unforeseen challenges while staying focused on the end goal.

Allocating Resources and Responsibilities

Ensuring Teams, Tools, and Timelines Are Aligned for Smooth Execution

Allocating resources and responsibilities is an essential step in the planning phase of the PDCA cycle to ensure the problem-solving process runs efficiently. The success of any plan depends on the clarity of the objectives and the effective allocation of resources, tools, and personnel. With proper alignment, even the most well-designed solutions can succeed during execution.

Defining Resources and Responsibilities

Resources in this context refer to the necessary tools, equipment, and materials required to implement a solution, while responsibilities refer to assigning tasks to individuals or teams. Both aspects must clarify who handles specific actions and what resources will be available to complete the tasks.

When resources and responsibilities are allocated effectively, the team is better equipped to complete tasks on time, without unnecessary delays. Aligning resources and responsibilities with the overall objectives makes the problem-solving process more structured, reducing the likelihood of miscommunication and inefficiencies.

Steps in Allocating Resources and Responsibilities

1. Assessing Resource Requirements
The first step in allocating resources is to assess what will be needed for successful execution. This includes identifying the tools, equipment, and materials required for each task. For example, if a solution involves upgrading software, the licenses, training materials, and hardware compatibility must be considered. It is essential to ensure that these resources are available and accessible to the team before implementation begins. Any resource gaps should be identified early so alternative solutions can be found.

2. Assigning Clear Responsibilities
After determining the resources, specific individuals or teams must be assigned responsibilities. Each task should have a designated owner who is accountable for its completion. Clear roles help prevent confusion and ensure that every team member understands what is expected of them. The person or team responsible for a task must have the required skills and experience to carry it out effectively. If additional training or support is needed, it should be provided before the task begins.

3. Creating a Timeline
A realistic timeline should be established for each task. Setting deadlines ensures tasks are completed promptly and that progress can be tracked throughout the execution phase. Timelines should account for the complexity of the tasks, resource availability, and potential obstacles. Milestones can be incorporated into the timeline to provide checkpoints for reviewing progress and making necessary adjustments.

4. Balancing Resources and Workload
It is essential to ensure that resources are dispersed across the team and that no one is overwhelmed by too many tasks. A balanced workload helps maintain team morale and productivity. Teams should be given sufficient time and resources to complete their assigned tasks without compromising quality. The process can stay on track by reviewing, allocating resources, and adjusting as needed.

5. Communicating the Plan
Once resources and responsibilities have been allocated, it is crucial to communicate the plan clearly to all team members. Everyone involved should fully understand their role, the resources available, and the completion timeline. Regular communication is critical to maintaining alignment throughout the process. Any changes to the plan, such as resource adjustments or deadline shifts, should be communicated promptly to ensure clarity.

Monitoring and Adjusting During Execution

During execution, continuous monitoring is essential to ensure resources are used effectively and responsibilities are fulfilled. Regular check-ins and progress reports help the team identify issues early and make adjustments as needed. If there are resource shortages, delays, or misalignments, the plan should be revisited and modified to address these challenges. Flexibility is key to ensuring that the project stays on course and that improvements are implemented successfully.

Risk Assessment and Contingency Planning

Identifying Potential Obstacles and Preparing Backup Plans for Successful Outcomes

During the planning phase of the PDCA cycle, risk assessment and contingency planning are crucial elements that significantly impact the effectiveness of problem-solving endeavors. Identifying potential risks early on and creating backup plans allows smoother execution and minimizes the impact of unforeseen challenges. By addressing obstacles in advance, teams can stay on track and achieve goals even when issues arise.

Importance of Risk Assessment

Risk assessment involves identifying potential obstacles, uncertainties, and threats that could affect the outcome of a plan. This process ensures that vulnerabilities are recognized and addressed before they become a key issue. Risks can range from resource shortages and technical failures to external factors, such as market changes or regulatory requirements. Understanding how these factors could impact the project is essential, regardless of the risk.

By conducting a thorough risk assessment, teams are better prepared to manage uncertainties and can plan for various scenarios. This step reduces the likelihood of unexpected delays or disruptions and increases the chances of a successful outcome.

Steps for Risk Assessment

1. Identifying Risks
The first step in risk assessment is identifying potential risks that

may impact the project. These risks can be internal, such as resource constraints or team conflicts, or external, such as regulation changes or supply chain disruptions. It is essential to involve all stakeholders in considering every risk. A comprehensive list of risks should be developed, focusing on areas that could directly affect the plan's success.

2. Assessing the Impact of Risks
After identifying risks, each should be evaluated based on its potential impact and likelihood. This evaluation helps prioritize risks and determine which ones require the most attention. High-impact risks should be given priority, and plans should be made to address these first. Medium- and low-impact risks should also be considered, but their likelihood and severity may require less immediate attention.

3. Developing a Risk Management Plan
Once risks have been assessed, a risk management plan should outline how each risk will be addressed if it arises. This plan should include specific actions to mitigate the risks and minimize their impact. For example, if a key resource becomes unavailable, a backup supplier or alternative method should be included in the plan to ensure that progress is completed on time. A plan for each risk reduces uncertainty and enables the team to respond more effectively when challenges arise.

Summary of Chapter 2: *Planning for Problem-Solving*

Planning is the cornerstone of successful PDCA implementation. This chapter details the importance of clear, measurable goal setting to guide problem-solving efforts. Specific goal-setting tools, such as SMART objectives, are explained to help create effective plans. This phase also involves identifying resources and responsibilities, developing actionable steps, and assessing risks to prepare for potential obstacles. Planning is a systematic process that lays the foundation for effective execution and reliable outcomes

Chapter 3: Executing with Precision

****

"Be the change that you wish to see in the world."

— Mahatma Gandhi

Implementing the Action Plan

Plan into action:

In the PDCA cycle, implementing the action plan is crucial, where plans and strategies are translated into tangible results. After identifying the problem, setting measurable goals, and developing a clear strategy, it is now essential to execute the plan systematically. Effective implementation ensures that the desired outcomes are achieved, making this step critical to the success of any improvement effort. This phase must be handled with precision and commitment to keep the process on track.

Step 1: Communicating the Plan

The first step in implementing the action plan is to ensure that all stakeholders are informed about the plan and their respective roles. Clear communication is necessary to avoid confusion and delays. Everyone involved should clearly understand the goals, timelines, and expectations. Aligning everyone with the objectives will better equip the team to work together toward a common purpose. This communication can be achieved through team meetings, written instructions, or project management tools.

Step 2: Allocating Resources

Once the plan has been communicated, the next step is to allocate the resources to execute it effectively. Resources can include workforce, budget, equipment, and time. Each task in the action plan must be supported with the appropriate resources to ensure smooth implementation. If resources are insufficient or unavailable, alternative solutions should be explored before moving forward. Careful resource allocation planning minimizes the risk of delays and ensures that the implementation progresses as planned.

Step 3: Assigning Responsibilities

With resources in place, assigning specific responsibilities to each team member or department is essential. A clear delegation of tasks helps ensure everyone knows what is expected of them, reducing confusion and increasing accountability. Everyone should clearly understand their role and how it contributes to the project's success. This step enables a more organized implementation, ensuring nothing is overlooked and that tasks are completed promptly.

Step 4: Executing the Plan

After roles and resources have been assigned, the plan is executed. This step requires a disciplined approach in which tasks are carried out according to the outlined schedule. During this phase, it is essential to follow the action plan and ensure that every step is implemented correctly. Deviations from the plan should be minimized, as they can lead to unintended consequences or delays. However, flexibility is also essential, as adjustments may be needed to address unexpected challenges. The focus should remain on executing each task efficiently while keeping the end goal in mind.

Step 5: Monitoring Progress

While the action plan is being executed, continuous monitoring is necessary to ensure progress. Regular progress checks help identify issues early, allowing corrective actions before the problem escalates. Tools such as progress reports, team meetings, and performance metrics can track the implementation's success. This ongoing evaluation ensures that the plan stays aligned with the initial objectives and that adjustments can be made when necessary.

Step 6: Making Adjustments

Unexpected challenges often arise during the implementation phase. If these challenges are identified during monitoring, adjustments should be made promptly. Adaptability is essential, whether it involves reallocating resources, modifying timelines, or revising responsibilities. Flexibility allows the team to address real-time issues, preventing the project from veering off course. It is important to remember that adjustments should be made thoughtfully to maintain the plan's overall goals.

Monitoring Progress in Real-Time

In the PDCA cycle, real-time monitoring of progress is vital to ensuring the successful execution of any action plan. Tracking tasks and performance as they unfold allows for timely adjustments, problem identification, and informed decision-making. Monitoring provides insights into how closely the process aligns with the plan and whether goals are being met. This approach is essential for achieving ongoing success in problem-solving.

Step 1: Establishing Key Performance Indicators (KPIs)

Before monitoring can begin, clear Key Performance Indicators (KPIs) must be established. These indicators help to measure progress and define what success looks like for each task. KPIs can include metrics such as task completion rates, resource usage, and timelines. By setting these benchmarks at the outset, performance can be tracked consistently throughout the execution phase. Specific, measurable KPIs enable teams to understand whether they are on track or need adjustments.

Step 2: Using Technology for Real-Time Tracking

Using technology is highly recommended to facilitate real-time monitoring. Project management software, dashboards, and tracking tools provide instant access to data, ensuring that tasks are tracked without delay. These platforms allow managers and teams to quickly view progress, making it easier to detect potential problems early. Automation tools can also be set up to generate reports on task completion, resource allocation, and overall performance. This streamlines monitoring while reducing manual oversight.

Step 3: Maintaining Regular Communication

Regular communication is crucial for effectively monitoring progress. Team members should be encouraged to provide updates on their tasks, share any challenges they encounter, and discuss potential risks. Scheduled meetings, daily check-ins, or instant messaging platforms can keep everyone aligned and ensure consistent progress reporting. Real-time communication ensures issues are identified as they arise, enabling faster responses and better decision-making throughout the execution phase.

Step 4: Reviewing Task Completion

It is essential to review task completion at every stage of the process. Monitoring whether tasks are completed on time and according to the plan enables teams to measure efficiency and make necessary adjustments. Delays or missed deadlines should be addressed immediately to maintain the overall timeline. Task completion rates provide insight into the effectiveness of resource allocation and the team's overall performance. This information is essential for making data-driven decisions and ensuring continuous progress.

Step 5: Analyzing Performance Metrics

Alongside task completion, performance metrics should be analyzed regularly. These metrics may include budget adherence, resource utilization, and productivity levels. Deviations can be identified and corrected by comparing actual performance with the initial plan. This analysis helps to ensure that the project remains on track and that any risks are mitigated. Using real-time data ensures that performance is tracked and optimized, enhancing the likelihood of success.

Step 6: Adjusting as Needed

Real-time monitoring enables adjustments when needed. If the data reveals deviations from the plan, resources can be reallocated, timelines extended, or additional support can be provided to address the issue. These adjustments help keep the project aligned with its goals even in the face of unforeseen challenges. Flexibility and adaptability are critical components of effective progress monitoring, as they allow the team to remain responsive and agile.

Ensuring Team Alignment and Accountability

Team alignment and accountability are crucial for successful problem-solving. Ensuring everyone understands their roles, responsibilities, and the project's overall goal helps create a unified approach. In the planning phase of the PDCA (Plan-Do-Check-Act) cycle, special attention should be given to aligning the team and holding members accountable for their tasks. When these elements are managed effectively, the likelihood of achieving desired outcomes increases significantly.

To begin with, each team member must know their role and the specific tasks assigned to them. Roles should be clearly defined during the planning phase to avoid confusion later. Each team member's responsibilities should be explained, ensuring everyone understands how their contributions fit into the plan. This clarity reduces the risk of execution overlap or gaps. In addition, clearly defined roles give everyone a sense of ownership over their work, enhancing accountability.

Open and consistent communication is essential to keeping the team aligned. By establishing clear communication channels, team members can stay informed about real-time progress, challenges, and changes. Regular updates, meetings, or check-ins can be scheduled to keep everyone on the same page. This ensures that any potential misunderstandings or misalignments are addressed early. Effective communication fosters a sense of collaboration and transparency, which are crucial to maintaining accountability.

The team should be aligned around shared goals that all members understand. These goals should be specific, measurable, and problem-solving-related. Setting clear targets gives team members direction, which helps maintain focus. When everyone is working toward a common objective, alignment follows. Shared goals foster a sense of collective responsibility, as each member understands how their contributions will impact the team's success.

Once roles and goals have been clarified, accountability must be assigned. This involves identifying who is responsible for each task and ensuring deadlines are met. Accountability should be built into the plan by assigning specific tasks to individuals or sub-teams, making it clear who oversees what. Regular check-ins should track progress and ensure that everyone remains on schedule. When accountability is assigned this way, monitoring individual performance and addressing delays or issues becomes more accessible.

Real-time progress monitoring is essential for maintaining accountability. Team performance should be tracked using metrics or milestones established during the planning phase. Feedback should be provided regularly to praise convincing performance and correct any deviations from the plan. This ensures that any misalignment is addressed promptly, keeping the project on course. Providing constructive feedback also helps to improve team dynamics and motivates members to stay focused on their responsibilities.

Accountability does not rest solely on individuals; the team should be encouraged to collaborate and support each other. Team alignment is reinforced when members collaborate, share ideas, and offer help when needed. Collaboration creates a sense of shared ownership over the project. It leads to stronger accountability because members feel responsible for their tasks and the team's success.

Overcoming Obstacles During Execution

Challenges are inevitable during the execution phase of any problem-solving process. Identifying and managing these obstacles in real time is crucial to ensuring the plan's success. Effective strategies must be in place to address unexpected issues quickly and efficiently.

One of the first steps in overcoming obstacles is ensuring continuous progress monitoring. This allows challenges to be identified early before they escalate into more significant problems. When potential roadblocks are detected, they should be assessed to determine their cause. This real-time identification enables swift action and keeps the project moving forward.

Flexibility in the plan is also essential. Although the planning phase strives to account for every scenario, unforeseen issues may still arise. The team should be prepared to adjust as needed to handle such challenges. This could involve reallocating resources, modifying tasks, or changing timelines to accommodate the current situation. A flexible approach ensures that the project can adapt without significant disruption.

Communication within the team plays a vital role in managing obstacles. When challenges arise, they must be communicated to all relevant team members to ensure alignment. Collaboration between team members should be encouraged to brainstorm potential solutions. By leveraging the team's expertise, obstacles can be resolved more efficiently.

Contingency plans developed in the planning phase should be implemented if necessary. These backup strategies ensure a smooth transition when challenges arise, minimizing delays and negative impacts on the plan.

Obstacles can be managed effectively during execution by monitoring progress, maintaining flexibility, fostering communication, and using contingency plans. Taking action early helps us stay on track and reach our goals, even when things get tough.

Maintaining Focus on Key Objectives

Maintaining focus on key objectives is essential to ensuring the success of any project or problem-solving process. During execution, distractions or additional tasks can arise, leading to a loss of direction. To prevent this, the team must remain committed to the original goals.

A clear understanding of the primary objectives should be established from the beginning. These goals must be revisited regularly to ensure that all actions and decisions align with the desired outcomes. Reminding the team of these objectives ensures consistency in the initial plan.

Potential distractions or new opportunities should be evaluated. While they may seem appealing, they must be weighed against the core goals to determine if they add value or divert resources. If the new tasks do not directly contribute to the primary objectives, they should be set aside for future consideration.

Regular progress reviews can be implemented to assess whether the team is on track to meet its goals. Any signs of misalignment should be addressed immediately, and corrective actions should be taken to return focus to the original plan.

By staying focused on the key objectives and avoiding distractions, the project will be more likely to achieve successful outcomes without unnecessary delays or resource strain. Maintaining commitment to the primary goals ensures that the problem-solving process remains efficient and effective.

Summary of Chapter 3: *Effective Execution in the Do Phase*

Execution is critical for turning plans into actions. The *Do* phase focuses on implementing the strategies outlined in the *Plan* phase, ensuring that each task aligns with the established goals. This chapter offers guidance on breaking down complex solutions into manageable tasks, assigning responsibilities, and setting timelines to keep the team on track. Real-time monitoring is emphasized to allow adjustments, enabling teams to respond quickly to unforeseen issues. Practical tips for maintaining team alignment and accountability during execution are provided to streamline the process.

Chapter 4: Measuring Performance

****

"If You Can't Measure It, You Can't Improve It."

— Peter Drucker

Defining Key Performance Indicators (KPIs)

Progress must be measured accurately to ensure goals are met in any improvement process. Defining the right Key Performance Indicators (KPIs) is crucial in evaluating whether actions lead to desired outcomes. KPIs provide a framework for tracking success and making data-driven adjustments to achieve the best results. By carefully selecting KPIs, teams can measure improvement and make well-informed decisions.

The following five KPIs are used to track progress in a continuous improvement process:

1. Efficiency Rate
The Efficiency Rate measures how effectively resources, such as time and labor, energy, and machine, are used to produce the desired output. It is a metric that focuses on process productivity and is especially useful in operational settings where time and resource optimization are key goals. The Efficiency Rate can be calculated by comparing the actual output to the maximum output over a specific period. For example, if a team completes 90 of 100 tasks within a set time limit, it achieves an efficiency rate of 90%. Tracking efficiency enables teams to see whether improvements enhance productivity and optimize resource use.

2. Defect Rate (PPM or DPMO)
Defect Rate measures the quality of output by identifying the

frequency of errors or issues within a process. In manufacturing and service industries, maintaining a low Defect Rate is essential to customer satisfaction and operational effectiveness. This metric can be calculated by dividing the number of defective items by the total number of items produced, then multiplying by 1,000,000 to obtain a PPM/DPMO. A rising Defect Rate can indicate the need for process adjustments, while a declining rate signals improvement in quality and consistency. Monitoring the Defect Rate helps ensure that quality standards are consistently met.

3. Customer Satisfaction Score (CSAT)
The Customer Satisfaction Score is a KPI that gauges how well customer expectations are being met. It is measured through surveys, in which customers rate their satisfaction on a scale of 1 to 10. The average of these scores yields a CSAT score that reflects customers' perception of product or service quality. High CSAT scores indicate the team is successfully meeting customer needs, while low scores highlight areas for improvement. In continuous improvement, CSAT helps the team prioritize efforts in the areas that matter most to customers, leading to better long-term relationships and loyalty.

4. Cycle Time
Cycle Time measures the duration needed to complete a single process cycle, from start to finish. This KPI is crucial for tracking the efficiency and speed of a process, especially in project management and manufacturing. By calculating the average time required to complete tasks, Cycle Time provides insights into how quickly processes can deliver results. Reduced Cycle Times indicate that bottlenecks or inefficiencies are being addressed, while longer times may signal the need for process optimization. Regular tracking of Cycle Time ensures that deadlines and schedules are met, contributing to an overall efficient workflow.

5. Return on Investment (ROI)
Return on Investment measures the profitability or financial

benefits gained relative to the costs incurred. ROI is calculated by dividing the net profit from an initiative by the total investment, then multiplying by 100 for a percentage. This metric enables the team to assess whether resources are used effectively to achieve financial goals. Positive ROI shows that the investment has been worthwhile, while negative ROI signals a need for re-evaluation. ROI is a fundamental KPI in continuous improvement, as it highlights the financial value of efforts and helps prioritize resource allocation. If you are in a new organization or an organization struggling to survive, forget ROI and focus on *Cash Flow*.

Choosing the right KPIs involves clearly understanding the organization's goals and what is most critical to a process's success. Each KPI should directly align with specific objectives set in the planning phase. By selecting these KPIs, the team has reliable metrics to measure progress, make adjustments, and drive continuous improvement. Effective KPI tracking enables ongoing success, as data-driven insights guide actions and ensure results remain aligned with strategic goals.

Gathering Accurate Data for Analysis

In any continuous improvement process, obtaining precise, trustworthy data is essential. Accurate data provides the foundation for sound analysis, helps identify areas needing improvement, and enables meaningful decision-making. With reliable data, any attempt to measure progress or analyze results can lead to skewed insights and practical action plans. Therefore, understanding techniques for collecting data accurately is crucial to success in the PDCA cycle.

Specific practices must be followed to ensure data reliability. Careful planning is required before the data collection begins. First, the purpose of the data must be clearly defined. Knowing precisely what is being measured, why it's being measured, and how the data will be used is essential for aligning data collection efforts with project objectives. When the goals are clear, data can be gathered efficiently and without unnecessary complexity.

Standardized methods should be used for data collection. By employing consistent techniques, data is gathered uniformly, reducing variations and discrepancies that might otherwise lead to analysis errors. For instance, if customer satisfaction is measured through surveys, using the same questions and scoring system each time ensures meaningful comparisons.

Sampling methods play a significant role in gathering accurate data. A representative sample must be chosen so that the results accurately reflect the larger population or process being studied. Random, stratified, or systematic sampling captures a diverse and representative subset. This approach minimizes bias and improves the validity of the collected data.

Automation and technology can improve data accuracy. Automated tools and systems reduce human error by capturing data directly from equipment or processes. For instance, digital sensors can measure production output, while software tools can track quality metrics or time spent on tasks. Such technology ensures that data is recorded with precision and consistency. Data should be captured in real time, allowing immediate insights into ongoing operations. Real-time data helps promptly identify trends or deviations, which is crucial for proactive PDCA cycle decision-making.

Standardized forms and templates should be used where manual data collection is necessary. Forms with predefined fields make it easier to record information consistently, reducing the chances of misunderstanding or misreporting. Staff involved in data collection are also essential to ensure they understand pricing accuracy and follow proper protocols. Mistakes or variations can be minimized when everyone knows the correct procedures and understands their role.

Data validation techniques should ensure quality before analysis begins. The validation process includes cross-verification with secondary data sources, data cleansing, and an outlier review. Outliers or anomalies should be examined, as they may indicate errors or provide insights into unusual occurrences. Cross-verifying data with reliable sources helps detect errors early, improving the integrity of the final dataset.

Confidentiality and ethical considerations are essential, especially when dealing with sensitive information. To maintain confidentiality, it is recommended that data be anonymized and storage systems secured. Ensuring that data is handled ethically increases trust and compliance with data-collection practices, leading to more accurate data collection.

The last aspect of gathering accurate data involves regular reviews and updates to the data collection process. Adjustments to the initial method may be necessary because of changes in the system or environment where data is collected. Continuous monitoring and improvement of data-collection techniques are required to ensure data remain relevant and reliable. By periodically reviewing these techniques, organizations can address data quality weaknesses and make necessary updates.

Accurate data collection is a structured and deliberate process that supports effective problem-solving within the PDCA framework. By planning, standardizing, automating, validating, and reviewing data collection techniques, organizations are positioned to measure performance accurately and achieve ongoing success.

Analyzing Results Against Goals

Assessing the effectiveness of any improvement plan involves comparing actual performance with the goals set during the planning phase. This analysis is essential for understanding how closely results align with expectations and for determining whether adjustments are needed. By systematically comparing outcomes with objectives, valuable insights into the impact of implemented actions are gained, which guide further steps in the PDCA cycle.

To begin the analysis, it is crucial to have clearly defined and measurable goals. These goals should have been set with key performance indicators (KPIs) that accurately reflect progress. Data gathered during the "Do" phase is evaluated against these KPIs. For instance, if the goal were to increase production efficiency by 15%, the actual production rates should be measured to determine whether the target has been met. The closer the results align with the goals, the more effective the implemented actions have proven to be.

Quantitative data is often used for such comparisons, as it allows a straightforward assessment of improvement. Production output, quality metrics, time efficiency, and cost reductions are quantitative measures that are easily compared to specific targets. For example, if the target were to reduce process time by 20%, time-tracking data would indicate whether the objective was met. If results meet or exceed the goals, the implemented actions can be deemed successful. If not, further analysis can identify the reasons behind the gap.

A practical approach in this phase is trend analysis. Observing performance over time identifies patterns and trends, which reveal whether improvements are consistent and sustainable. For example, an initial improvement that fades over time might suggest a temporary solution rather than a lasting one. Monitoring trends in key metrics helps assess the durability of improvements and determine whether further modifications are needed.

Visual tools such as charts and graphs can help compare actual performance with targets. A simple line graph, for example, can show actual outcomes versus expected outcomes over a defined period. Such visual representations make it easy to spot deviations and analyze their significance. If gaps between performance and goals are identified, it is beneficial to investigate these discrepancies to understand their causes. External factors beyond the team's control, such as supply chain disruptions, may sometimes impact results. In other cases, a closer look at processes might reveal inefficiencies that were not initially considered.

Root Cause Analysis (RCA) is often used when performance falls short of goals. Tools like the Fishbone Diagram or the 5 Why analysis help identify reasons for underperformance. By analyzing root causes, corrective actions can be developed to address specific issues. For instance, a targeted training program can be implemented to bridge this gap if insufficient training fails to achieve the goal.

When goals are exceeded, it is valuable to analyze why. Exceeding objectives can yield insights into successful practices that can be replicated in other areas. By figuring out what went well, we can learn from what worked and use those same methods to reach our goals more quickly in the future.

The final stage of comparing results with goals involves documenting the findings. Recording both successes and areas needing improvement creates a valuable reference for future PDCA cycles. Detailed documentation of each comparison, analysis, and the insights derived ensures that lessons learned are kept and applied in future efforts.

By carefully comparing actual performance with planned objectives, organizations can evaluate the success of their actions within the PDCA framework. The path toward continuous improvement is maintained by identifying gaps, analyzing root causes, and capturing lessons learned.

Identifying Gaps and Opportunities

A crucial part of measuring performance in any process is identifying gaps and opportunities for improvement. This stage in the PDCA cycle focuses on identifying discrepancies between actual outcomes and expected results, as well as areas for further improvement. Understanding gaps enables the opportunity to refine future actions and strengthen processes.

To begin with, it is essential to analyze the performance data collected in the previous phases in detail. This data is compared to the goals and objectives set during the planning phase, revealing where performance could have improved. For instance, if the aim is to reduce production time by 15%, but only a 10% reduction was achieved, this difference is a gap that requires investigation. Such gaps highlight areas where adjustments or additional resources may be needed to achieve complete success.

Using tools such as the Root Cause Analysis (RCA) can help effectively understand why these gaps exist. By applying methods like the 5 Whys or the Fishbone Diagram, the root causes of underperformance are uncovered. This analysis is valuable for identifying whether the gap is due to factors such as a lack of training, outdated equipment, or workflow inefficiencies. When root causes are identified, precise solutions can be crafted that address the specific issues rather than simply treating the symptoms.

Besides identifying gaps, attention must be given to recognizing areas of opportunity. Opportunities are often found where performance exceeds expectations or minor improvements can yield significant gains. For instance, if specific process improvements led to better-than-expected results, it might indicate the potential to replicate these practices in other areas. Analyzing what went right creates a blueprint for success, which can be applied more widely within the organization.

Benchmarking against industry standards or best practices is also valuable for identifying opportunities. Understanding how similar organizations or competitors operate can provide new insights and ideas for potential enhancements. This external perspective can offer fresh approaches to overcoming challenges and achieving higher efficiency.

Engaging the team in the analysis process can be highly beneficial, as those directly involved often have valuable insights into areas needing refinement. Gathering feedback through surveys, interviews, or group discussions allows employees to share firsthand observations and suggest potential improvements. Their experience can illuminate issues that may not be clear in the data alone.

Opportunities to improve are only sometimes related to problems; they can also include areas where proactive adjustments can further optimize the process. For example, upgrading technology, improving communication channels, or enhancing training programs are all potential areas for positive change that don't arise from a performance gap. These proactive opportunities enable continuous development, allowing the organization to stay competitive and efficient.

Once gaps and opportunities have been defined, it is essential to document these findings. This documentation serves as a reference for future PDCA cycles, ensuring lessons learned are preserved. The gaps identified, their causes, and the strategies to address them should all be recorded to create a comprehensive view of the improvement process. Capturing opportunities for improvement can guide future actions, ensuring that each PDCA cycle builds on the progress of the previous one.

In summary, identifying gaps and opportunities within the PDCA cycle enables an organization to make targeted improvements and advance toward its objectives more effectively. Refined actions can be implemented by analyzing discrepancies, understanding root causes, and recognizing areas for growth, leading to continuous success and resilience. A commitment to this analysis and refinement strengthens the organization's capacity for ongoing improvement, setting the stage for future achievements.

Using Feedback for Continuous Improvement

Feedback is vital in the PDCA cycle, especially for continuous improvement. When feedback is systematically gathered from performance data, valuable insights are provided into successes and areas that need further refinement. Using this feedback to inform each subsequent PDCA cycle establishes a foundation for ongoing growth.

Performance data is assessed in PDCA's "Check" phase to determine how closely outcomes align with initial objectives. Any gaps or unexpected results are reviewed to identify opportunities for process improvement. Feedback from team members, stakeholders, and even customers should be incorporated to build a well-rounded view of the performance. When this information is analyzed, it becomes clear where adjustments can be made, whether through process changes, resource allocation, or communication improvements.

Once areas for improvement are identified, this feedback should be organized and documented to ensure it can be easily referenced in future cycles. Clear, concise records make it simple to revisit past cycles, understand the changes made, and evaluate their impact. This approach allows teams to see trends in performance, recognize recurring issues, and build on past successes.

Incorporating feedback into the "Plan" phase of the next PDCA cycle completes the continuous improvement loop. With each cycle, lessons learned from previous feedback can avoid repeated issues and enhance efficiency. By consistently leveraging feedback, organizations can develop and refine their processes and drive sustainable growth. Thus, feedback is not just data; it becomes the engine that fuels progress toward excellence.

Summary of Chapter-4: *Measuring Performance*

The *Check* phase evaluates results against the goals set in the planning stage. This chapter highlights how to define key performance indicators (KPIs) and collect accurate data to gauge success. Various data collection techniques are explored to ensure reliable measurements, and tools for real-time monitoring are discussed to enable responsive adjustments. By analyzing outcomes, organizations can determine the effectiveness of their strategies, identify gaps, and recognize opportunities for improvement. This phase reinforces the PDCA cycle's emphasis on learning from results and making data-driven decisions.

Chapter 5: Learning and Adapting

****

"Intelligence is the ability to adapt to change."

— Stephen Hawking

Analyzing What Worked and What Didn't

Analyzing successes and setbacks uncovers valuable insights into every project or process. This process, essential to the PDCA cycle's "Act" phase, allows organizations to understand what worked well and what didn't, guiding improvements in future cycles. By methodically reviewing outcomes, patterns emerge that can strengthen strategies and prevent recurring issues.

Successes are first reviewed to understand the factors that contribute to positive outcomes. Analyzing these successes involves identifying which actions, tools, or strategies directly impacted the desired results. For instance, if a new process improvement led to increased efficiency, the elements that enabled it should be recognized and documented. Organizations can identify effective strategies to replicate in future cycles by examining specific techniques, team collaboration, and effective resource allocation. Successful actions are benchmarks, setting standards for future initiatives.

Failures reveal areas that need improvement. Analyzing setbacks requires looking beyond the surface to uncover root causes, enabling one to understand why specific actions didn't produce expected results. For example, suppose a new process failed to deliver anticipated efficiencies. In that case, whether it was due to insufficient resources, a misunderstanding of the task requirements, or a lack of team alignment should be determined.

By identifying these root causes, actionable insights are gained, enabling plans to be adjusted to address these weaknesses.

Gathering team members' feedback and insights is vital to success and failure analysis. Team members often hold unique perspectives on what worked and what didn't in the process. Their input should be gathered through structured debrief sessions, anonymous surveys, or open discussions, all of which encourage honest reflection. When these insights are documented and shared, they contribute to a more comprehensive understanding of each outcome, enriching the learning experience.

Organizing these lessons in a structured way ensures they are readily accessible for future reference. Documentation of successful strategies identifies weaknesses and suggests adjustments, creating a "lesson learned" repository. Each new PDCA cycle can then begin with a review of previous lessons, building on experiences to develop more informed plans. This organized approach reinforces the learning process and promotes a culture of accountability, as teams can see how each phase builds upon the previous one.

Finally, both positive and negative outcomes offer pathways for continuous improvement. The key to effectively closing the feedback loop is the commitment to regularly reviewing and applying these lessons. A thorough analysis enables organizations to move forward confidently, with a clearer understanding of what drives success and a proactive approach to avoiding past pitfalls.

Ultimately, the analysis of what worked and what didn't serve as a foundation for a resilient, adaptable organization. Continuous learning, rooted in these lessons, enables a culture where improvement is not only encouraged but systematically integrated into each cycle. By embedding this mindset, teams are positioned for growth, capable of adapting to developing challenges, and consistently driving the organization towards ongoing success.

Adapting Strategies for Improvements

Adapting strategies to ensure continuous improvement is essential in the PDCA cycle. By adjusting plans based on insights, an organization strengthens its approach, enhances efficiency, and increases the likelihood of achieving desired outcomes. Learning from each cycle in a structured manner helps maintain momentum in ongoing success.

In the "Act" phase of the PDCA cycle, an organization's experiences are analyzed to identify where strategies succeeded and where adjustments are needed. Patterns in performance are observed, and these insights are applied to refine methods or adjust objectives. The insights from the recent cycle reveal underlying strengths and weaknesses, enabling the development of targeted strategies. For example, if a project's implementation phase encounters a delay due to resource shortages, adjustments to resource allocation are made to prevent similar issues in future cycles. Every finding, whether positive or negative, contributes to enhancing plans.

When specific areas for improvement are identified, strategies should be revised to address them. This includes setting new objectives, adjusting resource allocations, or changing team structures to better align with goals. For instance, if team collaboration is insufficient, a new plan may emphasize communication protocols or structured check-ins to enhance coordination. The change approach is always rooted in making each cycle more productive and impactful. The organization can achieve more efficient, practical results by making targeted adjustments.

Insights from the PDCA cycle are documented to ensure all team members are aware of the improvements made. Documentation promotes transparency and ensures that future teams can easily access these learnings, preventing similar challenges from recurring. A structured documentation process helps create a learning repository for quick reference and onboarding new team members. Reviewing this knowledge base regularly ensures that lessons from past cycles are embedded in future processes. In this way, a clear framework for learning and adaptation is established, enhancing the organization's ability to improve continuously.

Feedback from team members is valuable when adapting strategies. Teams are often aware of specific challenges encountered and adjustments that would have been beneficial. Their feedback should be gathered through debriefs, surveys, or direct discussions, and they should be involved in shaping future strategies. When team members' perspectives are considered, the organization gains a well-rounded understanding of the improvements. This also promotes a sense of ownership and engagement among team members, as they see their contributions positively impacting the organization's progress.

Setting measurable goals in line with the adopted strategies helps maintain focus on the desired outcomes. Performance indicators and milestones are established based on changes, allowing the team to track improvements. Regular monitoring of these metrics ensures that adjustments continue to provide positive results and that any needed refinements are made promptly. This approach supports a proactive mindset, in which goals are continuously assessed against actual performance and further adjustments are made to sustain progress.

Adapting strategies based on insights gained from the PDCA cycle is essential for sustained success. The organization ensures that every cycle builds on the previous one by revising plans thoughtfully, documenting findings, gathering team feedback, and setting measurable goals. This continuous learning and adaptation process creates a solid foundation for ongoing improvement, enabling the organization to respond effectively to challenges and maximize growth opportunities. Through this commitment to refinement, the PDCA cycle becomes more than a tool for problem-solving; it transforms into a catalyst for long-term success and resilience.

Integrating Feedback into Future Cycles

Feedback is essential for refining processes and enhancing performance in every PDCA cycle. By integrating feedback effectively, an organization ensures that each cycle builds on the lessons learned, leading to continuous improvement and more robust results.

Feedback from the previous cycle should be carefully reviewed, with insights applied to address areas for improvement. This feedback provides valuable information on what succeeded, what challenges were encountered, and where adjustments may be required. Specific steps or decisions that proved effective should be reinforced in future cycles, while those that hindered progress are adjusted or replaced with more suitable alternatives. This approach ensures the organization grows by retaining strengths and addressing weaknesses.

Goals, processes, or resources should be adjusted to use feedback effectively. For instance, if a particular phase of the project encountered delays because of inadequate resource allocation, a plan can be put in place to allocate resources more effectively. Similarly, if team members provide suggestions for improved communication, structured channels can ensure clarity and reduce the risk of miscommunication in the next cycle.

The impact of each change should be tracked to determine its effectiveness. Performance indicators allow progress to be monitored, and any needed refinements can be implemented quickly, maintaining flexibility within the PDCA cycle.

In summary, integrating feedback into future cycles strengthens the organization's ability to adapt and improve. Through consistent learning and refinement, performance improves, challenges are managed more effectively, and each cycle contributes to long-term success. This commitment to feedback-driven improvement creates a dynamic process that keeps the organization moving forward, one cycle at a time.

Fostering a Culture of Continuous Learning

A culture of continuous learning is vital for organizations aiming to succeed in a changing environment. By encouraging teams to embrace learning and adapt to change, organizations can build resilience and foster growth. When individuals within the organization are motivated to gain new skills, reflect on their experiences, and adapt, they contribute to an atmosphere of ongoing improvement. Three strategies that can help establish a culture of continuous learning are outlined below.

1. Encouraging Open Feedback and Reflection

Creating a culture of continuous learning begins with actively encouraging open feedback. Teams should be supported in reflecting on their experiences and discussing what went well and where there may be room for improvement. Feedback sessions should be conducted to promote constructive dialogue and foster mutual respect. Team members can be asked to share insights into their performance, highlighting achievements and areas for improvement. The organization facilitates open discussions and ensures that learning from successes and setbacks becomes a regular practice.

Reflection can also be supported through structured activities like after-action reviews or debriefing sessions. These sessions provide an opportunity to pause, analyze outcomes, and document valuable insights. When consistently encouraged, this reflective process will reinforce the habit of learning from every project, initiative, or routine task.

2. Providing Learning Resources and Development Opportunities

Access to resources and development opportunities must be prioritized to build a strong culture of continuous learning. Employees are more likely to embrace learning when they have access to relevant training materials, workshops, or online courses. By offering resources such as e-learning platforms, specialized skill-training programs, or even peer-to-peer knowledge-sharing sessions, the organization signals a commitment to learning and growth.

Mentorship programs can also be highly effective, pairing experienced team members with those looking to expand their skills or knowledge. This exchange benefits the mentees and allows mentors to reflect on their expertise and gain new perspectives. Encouraging employees to attend conferences, webinars, or external training programs further fosters professional development and can bring innovative ideas and insights back to the organization. When learning opportunities are actively supported, teams feel more empowered and motivated to adapt to change.

3. Recognizing and Rewarding Learning Initiatives

Recognition is a powerful tool in establishing a culture that values learning. Teams and individuals who invest time in learning and show adaptability should be recognized for their efforts. This recognition may be informal, such as a verbal acknowledgment in a team meeting, or more formal through performance reviews or learning-oriented awards. When learning and improvement efforts are visibly valued, employees feel encouraged to continually pursue growth.

Rewarding learning initiatives can be as simple as allowing dedicated learning hours within the work week or offering small incentives for completed training courses. Recognition should also focus on adaptability—those who apply new insights to overcome challenges or streamline processes should be appreciated for their contribution. This approach reinforces that learning is essential to success and directly contributes to the organization's goals.

In summary, fostering a culture of continuous learning through open feedback, development resources, and recognition creates an environment where learning is encouraged and celebrated. When supported in learning and adapting, teams become better able to meet challenges and drive progress. Through these strategies, organizations can embed a continuous-improvement mindset, where each team member feels invested in their own growth and the organization's ongoing success.

Scaling Lessons Across the Organization

To maximize the impact of lessons learned, insights gained during the PDCA cycle must be shared across teams and departments. Scaling these lessons throughout the organization can expand improvements and enhance overall effectiveness. This process ensures that the benefits of valuable experiences extend beyond a single team or project, fostering a culture of shared learning and continuous improvement.

To achieve this, a structured approach is recommended. After-action reviews and documented lessons learned should be compiled in accessible formats, such as reports, presentations, or digital knowledge bases. These resources should then be shared through regular inter-departmental meetings, workshops, or team briefings, allowing insights to be discussed and adapted for broader application. Each team is encouraged to review these insights and assess their relevance to their projects or workflows. By adopting this approach, the organization ensures that knowledge gained in one area can inform the practices of others.

Standardizing communication channels for sharing lessons is also beneficial. Platforms like collaborative intranets or project management software can serve as central repositories for lessons learned. When insights are easily accessible, teams are more likely to review and implement them in relevant contexts. Training sessions, cross-departmental initiatives, and team-led presentations further encourage the spread of effective practices across the organization.

Scaling lessons requires commitment but offers considerable value. When insights are systematically shared, the organization becomes more agile and better able to sustain improvements across all levels. In this way, the benefits of the PDCA cycle extend beyond individual projects, promoting a culture where continuous learning and adaptation are fully embedded in the organizational framework.

Summary of Chapter 5: *Learning and Adapting*

The *Act* phase of the PDCA cycle is where continuous improvement takes shape. This chapter explores how insights gained from the *Check* phase can refine strategies and adapt plans for the next cycle. By closing the feedback loop, organizations can enhance their processes, reduce waste, and drive growth. Strategies for applying lessons learned and techniques for fostering a culture of continuous learning and adaptation are provided. This chapter emphasizes the importance of prizing reflection and feedback as essential components of long-term success.

Chapter 6: Applying PDCA in Teams

****

"Coming together is a beginning; keeping together is progress; working together is success."

— Henry Ford

Building Team Alignment Around PDCA

Building team alignment around the PDCA approach is essential for achieving consistent results and fostering a culture of continuous improvement. When teams understand and support the PDCA cycle, they are empowered to work together more effectively, share responsibility, and achieve shared goals. Clear communication, shared understanding, and team engagement must be emphasized to ensure alignment.

First, team members need to receive a thorough introduction to the PDCA approach. Training sessions should be held to clarify the purpose of each phase—planning improvements, implementing actions, assessing outcomes, and refining approaches. During these sessions, examples and case studies can be shared to demonstrate the impact of PDCA in real-world settings. When team members see how PDCA has led to concrete improvements in similar situations, they are more likely to understand its relevance and value. This initial training will help establish a solid foundation and create a unified understanding of the PDCA cycle.

Once training is complete, communication strategies should be put in place to maintain alignment. Regular team meetings are suggested to discuss progress within each PDCA cycle phase. Each team member can be encouraged to share their insights, ask questions, and highlight any issues they encounter. Open communication creates a sense of inclusion, making team members feel their contributions are valued and heard. Effective communication makes teams better equipped to move through the PDCA cycle cohesively, as each member understands their role in the process and how it supports the overall objectives.

Specific goals should be established for each phase of the PDCA cycle to strengthen alignment. Clear and measurable goals give team members a sense of direction and purpose. For instance, in the planning phase, targets related to problem definition, root cause analysis, and strategy selection should be outlined. These targets can then be communicated across the team so that each member is aware of the expectations and can work towards them. When clear goals are set, alignment is achieved as each team member works towards the same outcomes, fostering a shared purpose.

Ownership and accountability are crucial to building team alignment. Each member should be assigned specific responsibilities within the PDCA process to create accountability. When team members are entrusted with individual responsibilities, they are more likely to remain engaged and motivated. Assigning ownership also ensures that all tasks are covered and no areas are overlooked. Regular progress check-ins can be held to review each team member's progress and provide guidance if challenges arise. Accountability reinforces alignment around the PDCA approach as each member takes responsibility for their part in the cycle.

The team's collective achievements should be celebrated to reinforce alignment and motivation. Recognizing small wins at each stage of the PDCA cycle can help build momentum and encourage continuous participation. For instance, if a new process improves efficiency in the planning phase, team meetings should acknowledge this success. The team gains confidence in the PDCA cycle by celebrating these achievements and boosting morale. When team members feel appreciated and see the positive impact of their efforts, they become more committed to the process.

In conclusion, aligning teams around the PDCA approach requires structured training, open communication, clear goals, assigned responsibilities, and recognition of achievements. When these practices are followed, teams become unified in their understanding and support of the PDCA methodology, making it easier to collaborate on improvement efforts. Through alignment, the team can apply the PDCA cycle consistently, efficiently, and with a keen sense of purpose, leading to effective problem-solving and ongoing success.

Defining Roles and Responsibilities

In the PDCA cycle, clearly defined roles and responsibilities are essential for smooth execution and consistent results. By assigning specific responsibilities to the team facilitator, team leader, and team members, the team can work cohesively and ensure that each stage of the PDCA process is managed effectively. Each role contributes uniquely to the success of the PDCA cycle, reinforcing collaboration and accountability.

Responsibilities of the Team Facilitator

The team facilitator plays a crucial role in guiding and supporting the PDCA cycle to ensure processes remain focused and team dynamics remain positive. Key responsibilities of the facilitator include:

1. **Coordinating PDCA Activities:** The facilitator is responsible for planning and coordinating the PDCA activities, ensuring that all steps are completed in sequence and that timelines are followed.

2. **Encouraging Participation:** Facilitators encourage every team member to share insights, ask questions, and contribute ideas, fostering a collaborative environment.
3. **Managing Resources:** Facilitators ensure that necessary resources, including data, tools, and materials, are available to the team at each PDCA cycle stage.
4. **Monitoring Progress:** The facilitator conducts regular check-ins to assess the team's progress, keep the team on track, and identify potential obstacles early.
5. **Ensuring Accountability:** By assigning specific tasks and following up, the facilitator ensures that each team member is accountable for their responsibilities and that deadlines are met.

Through these responsibilities, the facilitator creates a supportive environment, guiding the team smoothly through each stage of the PDCA process.

Responsibilities of the Team Leader

The team leader is tasked with taking a more direct approach to ensure that each PDCA phase is executed precisely and that team objectives are met. Key responsibilities of the team leader include:

1. **Defining Goals and Objectives:** The team leader clarifies the PDCA cycle's goals and ensures all team members understand the intended outcomes.
2. **Delegating Tasks:** The team leader assigns tasks to the team members based on their skills and expertise, ensuring that tasks are managed efficiently.
3. **Overseeing Implementation:** The team leader closely monitors the execution of tasks, ensuring that each step is conducted according to the plan and that any deviations are addressed promptly.
4. **Providing Feedback:** The team leader provides constructive feedback regularly, helping team members

adjust their efforts as needed and stay focused on the objectives.
5. **Reporting Results:** At the end of each cycle, the team leader compiles results and prepares reports for review, highlighting successes and areas for improvement.

Through these responsibilities, the team leader serves as the point of coordination and direction, ensuring that each PDCA phase progresses as planned.

Responsibilities of Team Members

Team members are responsible for executing the tasks assigned to them and contributing to the overall success of the PDCA cycle. Their responsibilities include:

1. **Completing Assigned Tasks:** Team members are expected to complete their assigned tasks on time and with precision, contributing to the project's overall progress.
2. **Collecting Data:** Each member is responsible for gathering relevant data and insights for the "Check" phase, ensuring that accurate information is available for analysis.
3. **Providing Input:** Team members offer input during discussions, contributing ideas and suggestions that could enhance the PDCA cycle's effectiveness.
4. **Identifying Challenges:** Team members report any issues or obstacles, enabling the team to adjust its approach as necessary.
5. **Participating in Reviews: Team members participate in reviews** at the end of each PDCA cycle, sharing insights on what worked and could be improved.

Role and Responsibilities Phase-wise

In the planning phase of the PDCA cycle, it is recommended that a team leader or facilitator be designated to guide the process. This individual oversees discussions, gathers relevant information, and coordinates efforts to accurately identify the problem. Team members should be assigned roles focused on data collection, analysis, and goal setting, ensuring everyone contributes to understanding the root cause of the issue. By delegating these responsibilities early, the team can approach problem identification in a structured manner, which lays a solid foundation for the rest of the PDCA cycle.

During the "Do" phase, roles that focus on implementing the planned actions should be assigned. Implementation leads should be chosen to oversee the execution of specific tasks or strategies. These leads will coordinate efforts, track progress, and address any challenges. Other team members can be assigned support roles, help implement the tasks, and report any observations. This setup ensures that each task is given adequate attention and resources, increasing the likelihood of successful execution. By clarifying responsibilities in this phase, the team can avoid delays and confusion, ensuring the plan is implemented accurately.

The "Check" phase requires roles focused on monitoring, assessing, and evaluating results. Data analysts or quality control experts are assigned to measure the outcomes against set goals. These individuals can collect data, conduct analyses, and prepare reports, enabling the team to compare the actual performance with the expected results. Other members can be assigned roles focused on gathering feedback, observing outcomes, and documenting insights. Clear roles in this phase allow the team to determine whether adjustments are needed, supporting effective learning from the process.

In the final "Act" phase, team members should focus on refining the solution based on the insights gained. A team member or group can be tasked with identifying successful aspects of the plan and areas that require improvement. Roles focused on documentation are essential in this phase, as all findings must be recorded accurately to inform future PDCA cycles. Team members may also be assigned to communicate findings across departments, ensuring the knowledge is shared and potentially scaled for broader impact. By defining roles here, the team understands how to integrate their findings and improve their processes continuously.

Another essential component of role definition in the PDCA cycle is ensuring accountability. Each role should be linked to specific responsibilities and outcomes, creating accountability for each team member. Regular check-ins can review progress and address challenges, reinforcing individual accountability and promoting collaboration. When everyone knows their role and expectations, tasks are less likely to be overlooked or duplicated.

Defining roles and responsibilities in each PDCA cycle phase is essential for smooth execution and effective results. Clarity of roles helps the team function cohesively, as each member knows their duties and how they contribute to the overall process. This structure ensures that each task receives proper attention, minimizes errors, and allows for a continuous flow of actions toward improvement. By assigning roles that align with each PDCA phase, the team can efficiently work through the cycle, achieving success and sustaining progress.

Facilitating Collaboration for Problem-Solving

Facilitating collaboration is essential for effective problem-solving in a team setting. Open communication and teamwork can address issues more effectively, leading to innovative solutions. The success of the PDCA cycle depends on cultivating a culture where individuals feel responsible and enthusiastic about tackling problems. A collaborative environment enables diverse perspectives, broadens understanding of problems, and allows solutions to be approached creatively and efficiently.

Creating an Open Communication Culture

An open communication culture is essential to facilitate collaboration. Team members should be encouraged to express their ideas and share their insights freely. This culture is achieved by fostering a supportive environment where all voices are valued and constructive feedback is welcomed. By encouraging open discussions, team members can feel empowered to share their unique viewpoints, which helps to identify the root causes of issues.

Open communication is vital for exchanging information and updating the team on progress and obstacles. When communication flows freely, misunderstandings are minimized, and alignment on objectives is ensured. Tools such as regular team meetings, online collaboration platforms, and feedback sessions can support ongoing communication within the team. These practices facilitate the exchange of ideas and strengthen teamwork.

Promoting Teamwork and Shared Responsibility

Effective problem-solving within the PDCA cycle relies on teamwork and shared responsibility. Each team member brings unique skills and perspectives, which, when combined, contribute to more comprehensive problem-solving. Roles and responsibilities are clearly defined in a collaborative environment, but contributions are also interdependent. Team members are encouraged to help one another, share resources, and coordinate their efforts to achieve common goals. By distributing tasks equitably, each member can focus on specific aspects of the problem while remaining involved in the overall process.

Shared responsibility also fosters accountability. When each member understands their role and how it fits into the bigger picture, commitment to quality and accountability increases. This approach strengthens team cohesion and reinforces a culture of support where everyone is motivated to contribute their best effort.

Encouraging Creative Problem-Solving Techniques

Encourage creative problem-solving techniques to enhance collaboration. Brainstorming, mind mapping, and root cause analysis are valuable in generating diverse ideas. Brainstorming sessions can be organized to enable each team member to suggest potential solutions without fear of judgment. Mind mapping helps visualize ideas and connect concepts, while root cause analysis focuses on identifying the underlying issues that must be addressed. These techniques encourage team members to be creative and consider innovative approaches to recurring challenges.

Innovative solutions are more likely to emerge through these techniques, and the problem-solving process becomes dynamic. Team members are encouraged to explore different perspectives and challenge assumptions, thereby deepening their understanding of the problem.

Fostering a Collaborative Mindset for the PDCA Cycle

To foster a collaborative mindset, it is essential to emphasize the PDCA cycle's role as a continuous improvement process. Collaboration should not end after a single problem is solved; instead, it should be part of an ongoing effort to improve processes and address future challenges. Team members should be reminded that their collaborative input is valued for individual tasks and the organization's overall success. Promoting a continuous improvement mindset encourages collaboration throughout each PDCA cycle, with team members participating at every stage.

Building Trust and Mutual Respect

Trust and mutual respect are vital for effective collaboration. In an environment where team members feel respected and trusted, they are more likely to share and support one another. Mutual respect can be built by acknowledging each team member's contributions and recognizing their strengths. Trust is fostered by creating an environment where mistakes are viewed as learning opportunities. In this way, team members feel safe taking risks and proposing innovative ideas without fear of criticism.

Facilitating collaboration in a team environment is a critical component of the PDCA cycle's success. Problem-solving becomes more effective through open communication, teamwork, shared responsibility, creative problem-solving techniques, and a collaborative mindset. Trust and mutual respect create a solid foundation, enabling team members to work harmoniously and support each other's efforts. When collaboration is encouraged, teams can address issues more comprehensively, leading to more effective solutions and a culture of continuous improvement.

Tracking Progress and Accountability

Tracking progress and ensuring accountability are essential to applying the PDCA (Plan-Do-Check-Act) cycle in teams. By monitoring team activities and establishing accountability mechanisms, teams are better equipped to stay on track, meet deadlines, and address challenges as they arise. Precise tracking and accountability allow for a more efficient, transparent PDCA cycle and create a structure that encourages responsibility among team members. This approach is crucial for achieving continuous improvement and refining processes.

Setting Clear Objectives and Milestones

Objectives and milestones should be clearly defined during planning to track progress effectively. Each goal should be specific, measurable, achievable, relevant, and time-bound (SMART), as this framework provides clarity and helps break down larger tasks into manageable steps. By establishing milestones, the team can periodically assess its progress, making it easier to identify areas that require adjustment. These checkpoints help maintain momentum and ensure everyone is aligned with the cycle's goals.

When milestones are set, teams have a clear roadmap to follow and can track progress more efficiently. Each team member understands the deadlines and expectations, fostering accountability and motivating them to work toward achieving the objectives.

Utilizing Project Management Tools

Project management tools are highly beneficial for tracking progress and accountability within teams. These tools, such as Trello, Asana, or Microsoft Teams, allow tasks to be assigned to specific team members and reveal deadlines and priorities. Using these tools, a record of each task's progress can be maintained, providing real-time insights into the team's activities.

These tools enable tracking progress, monitoring timelines, and allocating resources. Team members can post updates on their task status, keeping the team informed without requiring frequent meetings. Notifications and reminders in these tools help team members remain accountable for their tasks, ensuring deadlines and responsibilities are met.

Conducting Regular Check-ins

Regular check-ins are vital to monitoring team activities during the PDCA cycle. Depending on the project, these can be held as brief daily stand-ups or weekly progress reviews. During these check-ins, team members are encouraged to provide updates on their tasks, share any obstacles encountered, and discuss any needed adjustments.

These meetings maintain transparency within the team and provide a platform for collaboration. Regularly assessing progress can identify deviations from the plan early, enabling prompt corrective action. This process keeps the team on track and reinforces accountability by requiring each member to report their progress to the team.

Assigning Accountability and Ownership

To ensure accountability, tasks should be assigned with clear ownership. Each team member should know their responsibilities and the expected outcomes. When individuals understand their specific roles, they are more likely to take responsibility for their tasks and deliver quality work. Assigning accountability also empowers team members to take ownership of their contributions, knowing they play a direct role in the success of the PDCA cycle.

Accountability can be further strengthened by assigning team roles such as facilitators, project leads, or coordinators who oversee progress and address potential roadblocks. Each team member understands their part in the bigger picture by having designated roles, and responsibility is distributed more effectively.

Monitoring Progress through Key Performance Indicators (KPIs)

Using Key Performance Indicators (KPIs) is another effective way to track team progress and ensure accountability. KPIs provide specific metrics that help assess how well the team is performing against its goals. For example, completion rate, task efficiency, and deadline adherence metrics can be used to evaluate the team's effectiveness.

Celebrating Wins and Learning Together

Celebrating wins and learning together is essential to the PDCA cycle, helping teams stay motivated and focused on continuous improvement. Recognizing achievements and reflecting on lessons learned fosters a positive team environment that values success and growth. This approach strengthens team morale and reinforces the importance of recognizing every team member's contribution to the process.

Successes should be acknowledged immediately after each PDCA cycle. Recognizing accomplishments—whether large or small—provides a sense of satisfaction and reinforces the value of hard work. When wins are celebrated, motivation increases, and team members feel their efforts are meaningful. Acknowledgement can be given through various means, such as a team meeting, a personal note of appreciation, or a shared message on the team's communication channel. Celebrating these moments ensures that achievements are not overlooked and that positivity is maintained within the team.

Equally important is learning together from each cycle. Analyzing what went well and what could be improved helps the team understand strengths and address weaknesses. Each team member can be encouraged to share their observations during a review session. Open discussions should be held, allowing everyone to express insights into how the team's efforts impacted the overall outcome. Challenges encountered during the process should also be reviewed, with emphasis on solutions and strategies that could be applied in future cycles. This shared learning experience promotes a culture of continuous growth and improvement.

Besides learning from mistakes, it is helpful to identify successful strategies that contribute to positive outcomes. By understanding what led to success, these strategies can be repeated or refined for future projects. Sharing lessons strengthens knowledge and skills, making the team more prepared and efficient in upcoming cycles.

By celebrating wins and learning together, teams can foster an environment that values achievements and growth. This approach improves team morale and equips members with insights and skills that benefit the team in future PDCA cycles.

Summary of Chapter 6: *Applying PDCA in Teams*

Aligning teams around PDCA is essential for effective implementation. This chapter outlines how team members can collaborate to refine processes, solve problems, and achieve shared goals. Prizing clarity of roles is emphasized, ensuring each team member understands their responsibilities within the PDCA cycle. Techniques for fostering open communication and accountability are provided, along with strategies for celebrating achievements and learning from experiences together. The chapter encourages a collaborative mindset, strengthening teams' commitment to continuous improvement.

Chapter 7: Case Studies in PDCA

****

"A case study reflects real-world problems and their solutions, providing lessons that no theory alone can teach."

— Anonymous

Case Studies:

In this chapter of *PDCA for Ongoing Success*, the transformative impact of the PDCA cycle across various industries is explored through exciting case studies. Toyota demonstrated how to change production and efficiency through a simple system of planning, doing, checking, and acting. Amazon's use of the PDCA method was examined to reveal how delivery speed was improved, inventory management was optimized, and customer experience was enhanced. Starbucks' case study shows how PDCA applies to fostering a productive work environment for employees. Intel's use of PDCA is shared as an example of how product development was streamlined, enabling a reduction in time-to-market and increased innovation efficiency. Netflix's success shows that trying new things, seeing what works, making changes, and trying again is how to improve something.

Toyota: Revolutionizing Manufacturing with PDCA

Toyota used PDCA to revolutionize its manufacturing processes, ultimately creating the recognized Toyota Production System (TPS) that made it a leader in lean manufacturing. Toyota's systematic approach to problem-solving, waste reduction, and continuous improvement offers valuable insights into the power of PDCA when applied correctly and consistently.

Step 1: Planning for Improvement

Establishing Toyota's approach began with detailed planning. Toyota aimed to eliminate waste, improve efficiency, and streamline processes. To achieve this, Toyota defined clear goals and objectives within the PDCA framework, focusing on issues such as production bottlenecks, overproduction, and excess inventory. This planning phase required a thorough analysis of production processes, employee roles, and customer demand.

In the initial stages, Toyota examined existing production practices to identify inefficiencies. The focus was on optimizing workflow, reducing waste, and creating a culture of continuous improvement (known as *kaizen* in Japanese). This led to a key principle in the Toyota Production System, *Jidoka*, which emphasizes stopping the production line if an issue occurs to prevent defective products from advancing through the system. This principle laid the groundwork for Toyota's ongoing commitment to quality and efficiency.

Step 2: Implementing (Doing) the Plan

Once the objectives and potential solutions were identified, Toyota moved to the "Do" phase. Small-scale changes were implemented across production lines to observe their impact. By adjusting controlled settings, Toyota minimized the risks of large-scale disruptions while gathering critical data for analysis.

One of the early changes implemented was the introduction of *just-in-time* (JIT) production. Instead of stockpiling materials, parts were delivered "just in time" for assembly. This method helped reduce excess inventory and led to more efficient production, aligning supply closely to demand. Alongside JIT, Toyota introduced *kanban*, a visual scheduling system that further supported JIT by signaling when new materials were needed. These tools helped create a more flexible and responsive production system.

During this phase, Toyota empowered employees to engage in the process, encouraging them to identify potential improvements on the factory floor. Employees were trained to recognize issues immediately and to take action by stopping production if necessary. This proactive approach to problem-solving ensured that inefficiencies could be addressed promptly rather than allowing them to accumulate.

Step 3: Checking Results

After implementing the changes, Toyota moved into the "Check" phase to evaluate the impact of their actions. The results of each change were analyzed to measure effectiveness. Metrics like production speed, defect rate, and overall efficiency were used to gauge success. By comparing actual outcomes with expected results, Toyota could determine whether the implemented changes had met their intended goals.

For example, after implementing JIT, Toyota analyzed reductions in inventory costs and measured improvements in production flow. The Kanban system was reviewed to ensure that material flow matched production requirements without causing delays. By regularly reviewing these metrics, Toyota could verify that its changes contributed to overall improvements.

Another important aspect of this phase involved all employees in the review process. Toyota believed that every team member played a crucial role in maintaining quality. Employee feedback was sought and considered, and the process was reviewed comprehensively and inclusively. This approach helped Toyota identify gaps in the initial implementation and provided insights for future improvements.

Step 4: Acting on Lessons Learned

In the final stage, Toyota consolidated the findings from the "Check" phase and acted on lessons learned. This "Act" phase ensured that successful changes became standard practices and that new insights could be incorporated into future PDCA cycles. Toyota created a solid foundation for consistent performance improvements by institutionalizing effective methods.

Lessons learned from each cycle were used to refine processes further. For example, Toyota continuously adjusted the Kanban system to respond to variations in demand. If any inefficiencies were identified, they were addressed in subsequent cycles, creating an evolving system of improvements.

Toyota's commitment to continuous improvement also influenced its culture. Employees were encouraged to view the workplace as a learning environment. The company adopted *kaizen* as a core value, emphasizing small, incremental changes rather than large-scale overhauls. This culture of continuous improvement allowed Toyota to adapt quickly to changing demands and continuously refine its processes.

Outcomes and Impact on Lean Manufacturing

The consistent application of PDCA at Toyota led to impressive results, including reduced production costs, higher efficiency, and improved product quality. Waste was minimized as processes became leaner and more responsive to actual demand. As a result, Toyota set a new standard in manufacturing, with companies worldwide adopting lean manufacturing principles inspired by the Toyota Production System.

Toyota's application of PDCA also showed how continuous improvement could become embedded in an organization's culture. Toyota created an agile, innovative production system capable of adapting to new challenges by promoting a systematic approach to problem-solving and empowering employees at all levels.

Key Learning from Toyota's PDCA Implementation

Toyota's success with PDCA can be attributed to several key factors that offer lessons for other organizations:

1. **Clarity of Purpose**: Toyota defined clear objectives focused on waste reduction, efficiency, and quality, setting a solid foundation for improvement.
2. **Employee Empowerment**: By involving employees at all levels, Toyota created an environment where everyone felt responsible for quality and improvement.
3. **Systematic Problem-Solving**: The structured application of PDCA enabled Toyota to address issues methodically, reducing the risk of large-scale disruptions.
4. **Culture of Continuous Improvement**: By adopting *kaizen* as a core value, Toyota fostered a culture that valued incremental progress and constant refinement.
5. **Adaptability**: The PDCA cycle was repeated continuously, allowing Toyota to respond quickly to new challenges and opportunities.

Toyota's revolutionary adoption of PDCA transformed its manufacturing processes and set new industry standards. By applying each step of the PDCA cycle—Plan, Do, Check, Act—Toyota established a model for achieving high efficiency, quality, and adaptability. The success of the Toyota Production System shows the effectiveness of PDCA as a tool for continuous improvement and highlights the importance of a collaborative, proactive approach to problem-solving. Through systematic planning, structured implementation, rigorous evaluation, and the commitment to learning, Toyota achieved lasting success and became a global leader in lean manufacturing.

This case study illustrates the potential of PDCA to drive operational excellence when integrated thoughtfully into an organization's culture and processes. It provides a powerful example for companies striving to enhance efficiency and adaptability in a competitive environment.

Amazon: Enhancing Customer Satisfaction Through PDCA

Through the consistent application of PDCA, Amazon has optimized its delivery speed and inventory management and created a culture focused on enhancing customer satisfaction. The following exploration details how Amazon has used PDCA, step-by-step, to achieve remarkable success in these areas.

Step 1: Planning to Enhance Customer Satisfaction

Amazon became one of the customer-focused companies through its commitment to customer satisfaction. Amazon identified key challenges that could impact the customer experience, including delivery speed, order accuracy, inventory management, and website functionality. Amazon aimed to address these factors strategically within the PDCA framework by recognizing them as core drivers of customer satisfaction.

To improve delivery speed, Amazon set specific objectives, including reducing delivery times, expanding its delivery network, and ensuring products were available when customers wanted them. Inventory management was another focus area. Amazon sought to minimize stock-outs and reduce lead times by ensuring inventory levels matched customer demand. With these goals in place, Amazon developed a detailed plan to serve as the foundation for subsequent steps in the PDCA cycle.

Step 2: Implementing the Plan (Do)

Once Amazon's objectives were clearly defined, the company moved to the "Do" phase, where solutions were implemented to address the identified challenges. Key strategies were deployed to improve delivery speed, inventory management, and website usability.

To enhance delivery speed, Amazon introduced several logistical innovations. Fulfillment centers were strategically located near high-demand areas to ensure faster delivery times. The company also implemented a sophisticated logistics network, including partnerships with delivery services and its fleet of trucks and delivery personnel. By testing these strategies in specific regions, Amazon could assess their effectiveness on a small scale before expanding successful models across the entire network.

Amazon has adopted an advanced demand forecasting system for inventory management to better predict customer needs. This system analyzes purchasing patterns and other data to ensure that popular items are stocked while lower-demand items are ordered in smaller quantities to minimize excess inventory. A real-time inventory-tracking system was established, enabling Amazon to quickly identify items in short supply.

Website functionality was another area Amazon addressed in the "Do" phase. A series of improvements was implemented to enhance the user experience, including easier navigation, personalized recommendations, and optimized search functionality. Each change was tested and reviewed to confirm its impact on the customer's journey.

Step 3: Checking the Results

After implementing the changes, Amazon entered the "Check" phase to evaluate the effectiveness of each solution. This phase involved a rigorous review of key metrics related to delivery speed, inventory accuracy, and customer satisfaction. By comparing actual outcomes with the targets set in the planning stage, Amazon could determine the impact of each change.

For delivery speed, average delivery time, and on-time delivery rates were analyzed. Data revealed that fulfillment centers near major cities significantly reduced delivery times, and delivery fleet expansions improved on-time rates. Amazon also tracked customer feedback to assess satisfaction with delivery speed. By reviewing these metrics, Amazon could confirm that its logistical improvements contributed to faster, more reliable deliveries.

Inventory accuracy was measured by tracking stock levels, order accuracy rates, and back-order occurrences. Data from the demand forecasting system showed reduced stock-outs, showing that inventory was being managed more effectively. Customer complaints about unavailable items declined, further validating the impact of these improvements.

Website functionality was assessed through customer feedback, usage analytics, and conversion rates. Feedback showed that the navigation improvements and personalized recommendations were well-received, making it easier for customers to find products of interest. These insights confirmed the effectiveness of Amazon's website optimizations.

Step 4: Acting on Lessons Learned

The last step in Amazon's PDCA process was to act on the findings from the "Check" phase. Changes that proved successful were scaled up and integrated into Amazon's standard practices, while additional improvements were made based on insights gained during the review process.

For example, based on positive results from the fulfillment centers near urban areas, Amazon expanded this model across other key regions, improving delivery speed nationwide. The success of Amazon's demand forecasting system led to further investments in data analytics and machine learning, enabling even more accurate predictions of customer demand. This allowed Amazon to refine its inventory management, ultimately reducing waste and improving product availability.

Continuous website improvements were also prioritized. Amazon adopted a regular review process to ensure the user experience remained seamless and up to date. By consistently analyzing feedback and usage data, Amazon could maintain an intuitive, customer-focused website that met the growing needs of its users.

Long-Term Impact on Customer Satisfaction and Growth

Amazon's systematic application of the PDCA cycle has profoundly impacted its ability to satisfy customers and drive business growth. By prioritizing customer satisfaction in each phase of the PDCA cycle, Amazon has not only met but often exceeded customer expectations. Delivery speed, inventory management, and website usability have all been optimized, contributing to Amazon's reputation as a reliable and customer-friendly platform.

One key outcome of Amazon's approach has been a consistently high customer retention rate. By addressing customer needs directly and maintaining a flexible, adaptable system, Amazon has fostered loyalty and trust among its user base. This commitment to continuous improvement has played a significant role in establishing Amazon as one of the world's leading e-commerce companies.

Essential points from Amazon's PDCA Application

Amazon's success with the PDCA cycle highlights several principles that can serve as valuable lessons for other organizations:

1. **Customer-Centric Planning**: Amazon's emphasis on understanding and addressing customer needs provided a solid foundation for its PDCA initiatives. By focusing on customer satisfaction, Amazon ensured that each improvement aligned with its broader goals.
2. **Data-Driven Decision-Making**: Amazon used data analytics to make informed decisions at every stage of the PDCA cycle. Data from customer feedback, demand forecasting, and operational metrics provided insights that guided Amazon's actions.
3. **Incremental Testing and Scaling**: Amazon's strategy of testing changes on a small scale before rolling them out minimized risk and allowed for more accurate assessments of each initiative.
4. **Continuous Improvement Culture**: Amazon's approach to PDCA was not a one-time effort but an ongoing process. This commitment to improvement became embedded in the company's culture, enabling Amazon to adapt and refine its practices.
5. **Adaptability and Responsiveness**: Amazon's PDCA implementation firmly focused on adaptability, allowing the company to respond effectively to changes in customer demand and market conditions.

Amazon's journey to enhance customer satisfaction through PDCA demonstrates the power of systematic, customer-focused problem-solving. Using each phase of the PDCA cycle—Plan, Do, Check, Act—Amazon has created a robust framework for continuous improvement that has supported its rapid growth and strengthened its customer relationships.

The success of Amazon's PDCA implementation is a testament to the value of setting clear objectives, implementing thoughtful changes, measuring outcomes, and making data-driven adjustments. Through this approach, Amazon has optimized delivery speed, improved inventory management, and created an intuitive online shopping experience—all of which contribute to its status as a leader in e-commerce.

Amazon's application of PDCA is a powerful example for organizations looking to enhance customer satisfaction and operational efficiency. By adopting a structured problem-solving approach and fostering a culture of continuous improvement, companies can achieve sustainable growth and build lasting customer relationships. Amazon's experience underscores the potential of PDCA as a tool not only for solving specific challenges but also for driving long-term success and innovation.

Starbucks: Improving Employee Engagement Using PDCA

Starbucks is a prime example of a company successfully implementing the PDCA method to enhance employee engagement and customer satisfaction. By refining its training programs and fostering a culture of continuous improvement, Starbucks improved service quality and customer experience. This case study outlines how Starbucks applied each step of the PDCA cycle to create a productive work environment for its employees.

Step 1: Planning to Improve Employee Engagement

The planning phase began when Starbucks identified the need to improve employee engagement to enhance service quality and customer satisfaction. Feedback from employees and customers revealed several areas for improvement, including consistency in training, skill development, and employee motivation.

Recognizing that well-trained, motivated employees contribute to better service, Starbucks prioritized developing a training program to address these issues.

Clear objectives were set during this phase, including creating standardized training materials, promoting open communication, and establishing a supportive environment for new and existing employees. These objectives focused on increasing employee satisfaction, strengthening job-related skills, and fostering a sense of purpose among Starbucks' "partners" (employees). The goal was to create an environment where employees felt valued, supported, and fully equipped to meet customer expectations.

Step 2: Implementing the Plan (Do)

In the "Do" phase, Starbucks began implementing the plan's outlined changes. The primary focus was on updating and standardizing training programs across locations. Starbucks introduced a structured training curriculum that covered essential skills for all roles, from baristas to store managers. Each training program emphasized Starbucks' core values, company mission, and customer service standards, ensuring employees understood job expectations and the company culture.

Starbucks launched a "coaching" system to support new hires, in which experienced employees acted as mentors. New employees received direct training that familiarized them with daily routines, customer interactions, and operational tasks. This buddy system allowed new hires to ask questions, build confidence, and feel welcomed into the Starbucks community. It also provided seasoned employees with an opportunity to show leadership skills.

Training programs were also enhanced for existing employees, with Starbucks incorporating ongoing skill-building sessions.

Workshops on customer service, conflict resolution, and product knowledge improved job performance and built a sense of personal growth. Management staff underwent specialized training to develop leadership and communication skills, which further helped them create a supportive environment for their teams.

Step 3: Checking the Results

After implementing the new training programs, Starbucks moved to the "Check" phase, in which the effectiveness of these initiatives was assessed. This phase involved evaluating employee feedback, job satisfaction levels, and customer service metrics to gauge the impact of the innovative programs.

Data was collected through employee surveys, performance reviews, and customer feedback forms. Employees were asked to provide input on the clarity of training materials, the helpfulness of the buddy system, and their overall satisfaction with their roles. Starbucks tracked turnover rates and absenteeism as indicators of employee engagement. Elevated levels of satisfaction and reduced turnover suggested that employees felt more motivated and invested in their roles.

Customer feedback was another key measure in this phase. Starbucks collected data on customer satisfaction scores, service ratings, and overall experience. Improvements in customer satisfaction were observed, as employees were now better prepared to deliver quality service, handle customer concerns, and maintain a positive attitude.

Comparing these results with the initial objectives confirmed that the changes led to meaningful improvements in employee and customer satisfaction. Employee engagement increased as training programs became more streamlined, and service quality improved because of well-trained, motivated staff.

Step 4: Acting on Lessons Learned

In the last phase, Starbucks focused on sustaining these improvements and making further adjustments based on the lessons learned from the "Check" phase. Successful elements of the training programs were standardized across all locations, while minor changes were made to address any remaining challenges.

For example, based on employee feedback, Starbucks adjusted its training curriculum to include more specific customer service scenarios. This included mock customer interactions, during which employees practiced handling real-life situations, such as addressing customer complaints or accommodating special requests. This hands-on experience further empowered employees to handle challenging situations effectively.

Regular "check-ins" maintain the quality of the training program. Managers and trainers were encouraged to provide ongoing feedback, which allowed Starbucks to identify new training needs as they arose. Starbucks created brief training sessions to teach employees the best ways to do their jobs and the latest company rules. This ensured that everyone followed the same guidelines.

Starbucks is committed to fostering an inclusive and positive work culture as a key component of employee engagement. Managers were trained to recognize and celebrate individual and team achievements, and feedback channels were kept open to ensure that employees felt heard. Starbucks strengthened employees' sense of belonging and pride by acting on employee suggestions and recognizing their efforts.

Long-Term Impact on Employee Engagement and Customer Satisfaction

The consistent application of the PDCA cycle allowed Starbucks to transform its training programs and significantly enhance employee engagement. By investing in employee development and fostering an inclusive, supportive work environment, Starbucks experienced lasting improvements in service quality and customer satisfaction.

Because of these changes, employees felt more motivated and connected to Starbucks' mission, resulting in lower turnover, higher job satisfaction, and better customer interactions. Starbucks' ability to create a supportive environment empowered employees to take pride in their work, translating into a more enjoyable customer experience.

Key Learning from Starbucks' PDCA Application

Starbucks' success with the PDCA cycle offers several valuable insights for organizations seeking to improve employee engagement and service quality:

1. **Clear Objectives**: Setting clear, achievable objectives helped Starbucks focus its efforts and ensured that each phase of the PDCA cycle was aligned with its goal of improving employee engagement.
2. **Structured Training Programs**: By developing a standardized training curriculum, Starbucks could equip employees with the skills and knowledge needed to excel in their roles and provide quality service.
3. **Mentorship and Support Systems**: Implementing a buddy system and providing ongoing mentorship created a welcoming environment for new hires while giving existing employees leadership opportunities.
4. **Employee Feedback and Continuous Improvement**: Regularly gathering employee feedback allowed Starbucks to refine its training programs, ensuring they remained relevant and effective.
5. **Recognition and Positive Work Culture**: Recognizing employee contributions and fostering a

positive work culture strengthened engagement and reinforced Starbucks' commitment to its employees.

The PDCA cycle has proven to be a valuable tool for Starbucks in improving employee engagement and customer satisfaction. By applying the PDCA principles—Plan, Do, Check, Act—Starbucks has created a training program that enhances job performance and supports employee well-being.

Through thoughtful planning, continuous monitoring, and responsive action, Starbucks successfully built a positive work environment where employees feel valued and motivated. This investment in employee engagement has yielded tangible benefits, including improved service quality, stronger customer relationships, and a loyal workforce.

Starbucks' experience highlights the power of the PDCA framework for continuous improvement. Organizations can create an environment where employees and customers can thrive by setting clear goals, implementing strategic changes, evaluating outcomes, and refining processes. Starbucks' application of PDCA serves as an inspiring example of how businesses can build a supportive culture that drives long-term success.

Intel: Streamlining Product Development with PDCA

By implementing PDCA, Intel optimized its product development process, minimized delays, and enhanced quality, ultimately strengthening its position in the competitive technology sector. This section breaks down Intel's PDCA approach in product development and examines each phase's role in refining its processes.

Step 1: Planning for Efficient Product Development

Intel's commitment to rapid product innovation required a clear, structured approach to planning. The goal of the "Plan" phase was to outline a streamlined product development roadmap that would balance innovation with efficiency. Intel aimed to reduce delays, limit design flaws, and optimize resource allocation, recognizing that a well-thought-out plan would be critical to achieving these objectives.

During this phase, Intel established specific objectives:

1. **Reducing Development Time:** Setting a clear timeline to bring products to market faster.
2. **Minimizing Design Errors:** Aiming to reduce rework through early identification of potential flaws.
3. **Maximizing Innovation Quality:** Improving product performance, reliability, and user experience.
4. **Optimizing Resource Allocation:** Ensuring resources were effectively assigned to avoid bottlenecks.

Intel conducted market research to identify customer needs and emerging technology trends, ensuring the product design aligned with market expectations. The planning team worked closely with R&D, engineering, and marketing to establish specifications, design requirements, and a realistic timeline.

Step 2: Implementing the Plan (Do)

After defining a comprehensive plan, Intel moved to the "Do" phase. This phase involved executing the product development plan through a structured process that enabled regular testing and iteration. By breaking down the development into smaller stages, Intel could maintain quality control and adapt as needed.

Several steps were taken to ensure the successful execution of the plan:

1. **Prototyping and Iteration:** Intel developed prototypes based on initial design specifications. This enabled testing at an early stage, helping identify design issues before moving into development.
2. **Cross-functional collaboration:** Engineering, quality assurance, and R&D teams collaborated. Engineers worked on core functionalities while quality assurance teams tested and analyzed each component. Regular communication between departments ensured that feedback was immediately incorporated.
3. **Pilot Testing:** Initial product versions were tested to simulate real-world usage. This testing phase identified usability issues, functional gaps, and any deviations from design specifications.
4. **Resource Management:** Resource allocation was closely monitored to avoid delays. Intel used project management software to track resource availability, helping to ensure that each stage of development had support.

Throughout this phase, Intel maintained flexibility by adopting a responsive approach. If issues were detected, real-time adjustments were made to ensure progress remained on track. Regular status meetings allowed the team to align efforts and address emerging concerns, keeping the project focused on the core objectives outlined during the planning phase.

Step 3: Checking the Results

The "Check" phase involved evaluating the outcomes of the actions taken in the "Do" phase. Intel's project team reviewed performance data from the initial testing stages to determine whether the development process aligned with the planned objectives. This phase was crucial in identifying successes and areas requiring further refinement.

Intel's evaluation focused on several key metrics:

1. **Time-to-Market:** The time taken from concept to initial product release was compared with planned timelines. Any delays were documented and analyzed to understand their root causes.
2. **Error Rate:** The number of design flaws and errors detected during testing was reviewed. Intel aimed to identify the primary sources of errors and implement solutions to prevent them in future projects.
3. **Customer Feedback Simulation:** Intel conducted focus group testing on Prototypes to gather insights into customer satisfaction with product functionality and quality. Although the testing was performed on prototypes, the feedback provided valuable indicators of potential market reception.
4. **Resource Efficiency:** The effectiveness of resource allocation was assessed by comparing budgeted resources with actual usage. Intel analyzed resource bottlenecks and any areas where resource allocation needed improvement.

Data collected during this phase created a comprehensive report on the development process's strengths and weaknesses. Intel used these insights to guide the final "Act" phase, allowing the team to make informed decisions on adjustments and improvements.

Step 4: Acting on Insights for Future Improvements

The "Act" phase enabled Intel to integrate insights from the "Check" phase to refine and enhance its development processes. Lessons learned were documented, and steps were taken to improve product development for future projects.

Key improvements implemented included:

1. **Enhanced Quality Control:** Additional checkpoints were added at critical stages in the development cycle.

These checkpoints enabled earlier detection of errors and design flaws, reducing the likelihood that issues would reach later stages.
2. **Resource Reallocation:** Based on identified bottlenecks, Intel reallocated resources to improve efficiency. For instance, additional support was provided to the testing and prototyping stages to prevent delays in final product releases.
3. **Refinement of Prototyping Process:** Intel refined its prototyping methods to replicate the end-user experience better, allowing for a more accurate assessment of product performance during testing.
4. **Documentation and Knowledge Sharing:** Best practices and lessons learned from the project were documented and shared with cross-functional teams. This knowledge-sharing approach ensured that future teams benefited from prior experience, enabling continual improvement of the development cycle.

During the "Act" phase, Intel could institutionalize the identified improvements, setting the stage for ongoing process enhancement. By continually refining the development process, Intel maintained its competitive edge, launching products that met market demands efficiently and precisely.

Long-Term Impact of PDCA on Intel's Product Development

The consistent application of the PDCA cycle has significantly impacted Intel's product development process, fostering a culture of continuous improvement. By adopting PDCA as a core method, Intel achieved faster time-to-market, improved product quality, and more efficient resource allocation.

Through this structured approach, Intel could better meet customer expectations, reduce production costs, and maintain its leadership in the tech industry. The PDCA cycle has provided

Intel with a framework to remain adaptable in a changing industry, driving innovation without compromising quality or efficiency.

Key Learnings from Intel's PDCA Application

Intel's use of the PDCA cycle offers valuable lessons for other organizations seeking to optimize product development processes:

1. **Clear Planning Objectives:** Setting specific, achievable goals during the planning phase ensured that Intel's development efforts remained focused and aligned with broader organizational priorities.
2. **Cross-Functional Collaboration:** Close collaboration between departments facilitated a unified approach to problem-solving, ensuring that feedback was effectively integrated into each development stage.
3. **Continuous Evaluation and Adjustment:** By continuously evaluating progress, Intel could identify issues early and make timely adjustments, minimizing the impact of potential setbacks.
4. **Standardization of Best Practices:** Lessons learned were documented and shared across the organization, promoting a culture of knowledge sharing and continuous improvement.
5. **Customer-Centric Approach:** Gathering feedback from focus groups and simulated market testing allowed Intel to anticipate customer needs better and ensure that the final products aligned with market demands.

Intel's experience with the PDCA cycle shows the effectiveness of a structured approach to product development. Intel significantly improved its product development cycle by planning, executing systematically, evaluating progress, and adjusting insight-based processes.

The PDCA cycle enabled Intel to maintain high-quality standards, reduce development time, and better meet customer expectations. This case study highlights the importance of prioritizing a systematic, iterative approach to achieving sustainable growth and innovation efficiency. By embracing the principles of PDCA, Intel has set a standard for excellence in product development, serving as an example for organizations seeking to thrive in competitive, rapidly evolving industries.

Netflix: Continuously Enhancing User Experience with PDCA

Netflix, a leader in the streaming industry, applied PDCA to optimize its recommendation algorithm and improve content delivery. By focusing on these key areas, Netflix continuously increased user satisfaction and engagement, solidifying its reputation as a top streaming platform. This section will explore how Netflix implemented the PDCA process step by step to achieve its objectives.

Step 1: Planning to Enhance User Experience

To stay ahead in the streaming industry, Netflix prioritized enhancing user experience as a core strategic objective. The "Plan" phase focused on defining specific goals related to user satisfaction and engagement. To accomplish these goals, Netflix needed to optimize two primary areas: its recommendation algorithm and content delivery system.

The primary objectives of this planning phase were:

1. **Improving Recommendation Accuracy**: By enhancing the recommendation algorithm, Netflix aimed to ensure that users would receive relevant content suggestions, keeping them engaged.

2. **Reducing Buffering and Load Times**: Improving content delivery was another priority, as delays in streaming could disrupt the user experience.
3. **Personalizing User Interactions**: Netflix planned to enhance personalization by tailoring recommendations, homepage layout, and content presentation to individual preferences.
4. **Increasing Viewer Retention**: By creating an engaging and seamless experience, Netflix intended to boost viewer retention, a key metric for subscriber growth.

Data collection and market analysis were conducted during this phase to understand user behavior and preferences. The product team collaborated with data scientists, engineers, and UX designers to create a roadmap aligned with Netflix's overarching goals.

Step 2: Implementing the Plan (Do)

In the "Do" phase, Netflix implemented its plan by enhancing the recommendation algorithm and optimizing content delivery. This phase focused on incremental improvements through frequent testing and development cycles, ensuring that changes positively impacted user experience.

The implementation steps included:

1. **Algorithm Refinement**: Data scientists and engineers began by enhancing the recommendation algorithm. Machine learning techniques were used to analyze viewing patterns, content interactions, and user preferences, enabling Netflix to predict better what users might want to watch next.
2. **Content Delivery Optimization**: Netflix improved its content delivery network (CDN) to reduce buffering and loading times. By caching content in regional servers

closer to users, Netflix reduced lag and improved streaming speeds. The infrastructure team ensured high-quality content delivery remained consistent across locations.
3. **Personalization Enhancements**: Personalized user interfaces were tested to improve engagement. Netflix experimented with various ways to display recommendations, such as highlighting trending content and tailoring the homepage to viewing habits. A/B testing evaluated which layouts and designs resonated best with users.
4. **Incremental Updates and Testing**: Continuous A/B testing was conducted to ensure that changes positively impacted the user experience. By testing multiple variations, Netflix could refine the algorithm and user interface based on real-time feedback.
5. **Feedback Loop Establishment**: User feedback was gathered through surveys and performance metrics, providing the team with insights into areas requiring change. This feedback loop enabled Netflix to detect negative impacts early and adapt as needed.

Throughout this phase, Netflix maintained a flexible approach, implementing changes in small increments to avoid overwhelming users. Each update was tracked and monitored to ensure it contributed to the broader goals set in the planning phase.

Step 3: Checking the Results

The "Check" phase involved analyzing the impact of the changes made in the "Do" phase. During this phase, Netflix assessed whether the enhancements had met the desired objectives and whether additional improvements were necessary.

The evaluation process focused on the following areas:

1. **User Engagement Metrics**: The frequency and duration of user interactions were monitored to assess if the recommendation algorithm was generating interest. Higher engagement showed that users were finding relevant content more easily.
2. **Reduction in Buffering and Load Times**: By monitoring streaming quality and load times, Netflix evaluated whether improvements to the CDN were successful. A decrease in buffering issues and faster loading times were indicators of a successful implementation.
3. **Personalization Success**: Metrics, such as click-through rates on recommended content, session duration, and user satisfaction scores, were analyzed to evaluate the effectiveness of personalization efforts. User feedback was also reviewed to understand their responses to the updated recommendation system and UI design.
4. **User Retention Rates**: Increased viewer retention was a critical success metric. Netflix examined subscriber growth and churn rates to gauge the long-term impact of the PDCA cycle on user satisfaction.
5. **Continuous Feedback Review**: Surveys and focus groups provided qualitative insights into the effectiveness of the improvements. Users shared their thoughts on content relevance, ease of finding shows, and overall experience.

This phase allowed Netflix to identify successful changes and any remaining areas for refinement. By monitoring these key metrics, Netflix gained valuable insights to guide future cycles.

Step 4: Acting on Insights for Future Cycles

In the "Act" phase, Netflix used the findings from the "Check" phase to further refine its processes. Adjustments were made to enhance features and address any lingering issues, ensuring continuous improvement in the user experience.

Key actions taken in this phase included:

1. **Refinement of Algorithm Features**: Based on engagement data, some aspects of the recommendation algorithm were further enhanced. If specific content types (e.g., genres or formats) showed higher engagement, these were prioritized in future recommendations.
2. **Expansion of CDN Improvements**: The positive impact of CDN improvements prompted Netflix to expand these enhancements to additional regions. This decision helped ensure a seamless experience across a broader user base, particularly in areas with high subscriber growth.
3. **Personalization Adjustments**: Feedback suggested that some users preferred more control over recommendations, leading Netflix to implement features that allowed users to provide input on their preferences.
4. **Documenting Best Practices and Lessons Learned**: Successful strategies were documented as best practices, forming the foundation for future PDCA cycles. Lessons learned were shared across the development, data science, and product teams to ensure improvements were built upon for subsequent iterations.
5. **Setting New Goals for Upcoming Cycles**: New objectives were defined for the next round based on the successful outcomes of the current PDCA cycle. These goals aimed to drive further engagement and refine the user experience by incorporating emerging technologies and market trends.

Long-Term Impact of PDCA on Netflix's User Experience

Netflix achieved substantial long-term improvements in user experience and engagement by continuously applying the PDCA cycle. The recommendation algorithm became more accurate and relevant while improving the streaming quality. This iterative approach enabled Netflix to stay aligned with developing user expectations, making the platform more engaging and accessible.

Netflix's PDCA-driven approach has enabled the company to maintain a competitive edge in the streaming industry, setting a standard for continuous user experience improvement. The ongoing cycle of planning, implementing, evaluating, and refining has fostered a culture of data-driven decision-making and responsiveness to user feedback, helping maintain Netflix's reputation as a leader in user satisfaction.

Essential points from Netflix's PDCA Application

Netflix uses a PDCA system to improve the user experience, and other companies can learn from its method.

1. **User-Centric Planning**: Defining clear objectives related to user satisfaction ensures that improvements align with customer needs and preferences.
2. **Frequent Testing and Iteration**: Small, incremental changes allow continuous improvement without overwhelming users or disrupting the experience.
3. **Data-Driven Evaluation**: Monitoring key metrics helps organizations assess the success of changes and quickly identify areas requiring further attention.
4. **Feedback Integration**: Incorporating user feedback into the refinement process strengthens the overall quality and relevance of product features.
5. **Documentation for Continuous Improvement**: Documenting best practices and lessons learned creates a foundation for future cycles, supporting sustained progress and adaptation.

Netflix's use of the PDCA cycle underscores the power of structured, iterative improvement in enhancing user experience. Netflix has always tried to make its users happy by setting clear goals, making changes, checking how well those changes worked, and improving its methods. The PDCA approach enabled Netflix to respond to user feedback, minimize issues, and optimize its recommendation algorithm and content delivery.

This case study highlights the importance of prizing a user-focused, data-driven approach to achieving sustained growth and customer loyalty. Netflix's success with PDCA exemplifies how a systematic improvement cycle can transform a company's product offering, making it more engaging, relevant, and reliable for users.

Summary of Chapter 7: Case *Studies in PDCA*

Real-world case studies illustrate the practical impact of PDCA across industries. Each case study examines how a leading company successfully applied PDCA to address challenges, improve efficiency, and achieve strategic objectives. For example, Toyota's pioneering use of PDCA to enhance manufacturing efficiency is explored, showing how the cycle contributed to the company's lean manufacturing success. Other cases, such as Amazon's customer satisfaction initiatives and Intel's product development process optimization, demonstrate how PDCA can drive innovation and deliver results across different organizational functions. Each example serves as a roadmap for readers to understand how to apply PDCA effectively.

Chapter 8: Scaling PDCA for Growth

****

"Scaling is about making good decisions on the fly and doing what's right, not what's easy."

— Reid Hoffman

Expanding PDCA Across Departments

Focuses on scaling the PDCA cycle for broader organizational growth by applying it across departments. Expanding PDCA beyond individual teams can build a culture of continuous improvement, encouraging all parts of the organization to work toward shared objectives. In this way, improvements from small-scale applications can be scaled, resulting in impactful, organization-wide benefits. Here is a step-by-step guide for expanding PDCA across departments.

Step 1: Establish Organizational Alignment

Alignment with organizational goals is necessary to ensure effective PDCA use across departments. First, all departments should be introduced to the overall objectives and vision for improvement. Then, it should be clarified how each department's processes and outputs contribute to the larger goals. This alignment helps employees understand the relevance of PDCA to their work, increasing their likelihood of supporting and engaging with the cycle.

Step 2: Standardize PDCA Processes

Standardizing PDCA processes is essential to ensure that each department follows a similar approach. Clear guidelines for each step—planning, doing, checking, and acting should be documented. Training sessions or workshops can be conducted to equip departments with the skills and knowledge. Templates and checklists can also be provided to maintain consistency, making the PDCA cycle easier to implement and track across different areas.

Step 3: Implement Cross-Department Collaboration

Cross-department collaboration is critical when expanding PDCA. Departments must collaborate to share knowledge, resources, and successful practices. Collaborative meetings should be scheduled to discuss each department's progress and identify common challenges hindering PDCA implementation. By establishing a platform for open communication, departments can learn from each other's experiences, allowing improvements to be applied more efficiently.

Step 4: Set Department-Specific Goals and KPIs

Each department should have its specific objectives within the larger PDCA framework. Key Performance Indicators (KPIs) tailored to each department's unique functions are essential to tracking progress. These KPIs can measure improvements in quality, efficiency, or customer satisfaction. Setting department-specific goals will help ensure that PDCA efforts are relevant and impactful, contributing directly to organizational objectives.

Step 5: Monitor Progress and Share Results

Progress should be monitored regularly to assess each department's performance within the PDCA cycle. This tracking can be done through regular check-ins or data reports, which department leaders and stakeholders can review. Sharing progress reports and results across departments promotes transparency and allows successful practices to be replicated. Teams can gain insights into what works best, and departments that face challenges can receive support to improve their implementation.

Step 6: Apply Improvements Across Departments

Once results from one department show a positive impact, improvements can be applied across others. For example, if one department finds success with a particular approach to problem-solving, the same technique can be adopted by other departments. Scaling improvements in this way ensures that successful strategies benefit the entire organization, leading to a more cohesive and effective process across departments.

Step 7: Promote a Culture of Continuous Improvement

A culture of continuous improvement should be fostered across all departments. Leadership is key in promoting PDCA as a continuous, adaptive process rather than a one-time project. Celebrating wins and encouraging feedback help reinforce the value of PDCA, motivating teams to embrace the cycle consistently. By nurturing a mindset of ongoing development, the organization can stay competitive and responsive to changing needs.

Expanding PDCA across departments enables small-scale improvements to be leveraged organization-wide. By following these structured steps, an organization can create a unified approach to continuous improvement that positively impacts each department, ultimately driving sustainable growth and enhanced performance across the entire organization.

Standardizing Processes for Consistency

Emphasizing the importance of standardized processes, PDCA for Ongoing Success helps effectively scale the PDCA cycle across an organization. Standardized procedures bring consistency and ensure that the PDCA methodology is applied uniformly across teams and departments. When standardized processes are established, teams can more easily collaborate, measure progress, and improve efficiency. Below is a structured approach to creating standardized processes that ensure consistent PDCA application at scale.

Define Clear Guidelines for PDCA Application

To standardize PDCA, clear guidelines must be established for each cycle step. It should be clarified what "Plan," "Do," "Check," and "Act" entail within the organization's context. Examples of activities, tools, and expectations for each stage can be included in a documented PDCA framework. This framework will serve as a reference for teams, helping them understand the steps required and how to adapt them to different projects or challenges. By providing this structure, all departments can apply PDCA consistently.

Develop Standard Operating Procedures (SOPs)

Standard Operating Procedures (SOPs) for PDCA should guide teams in executing each phase effectively. SOPs can cover key aspects, such as project initiation, data collection, and analysis techniques, and even specify the frequency and format of progress reviews. These procedures should be easily accessible and well-documented, promoting team consistency. SOPs allow employees to reference the same guidelines, ensuring that PDCA is applied throughout the organization.

Use Templates and Checklists for Uniformity

Templates and checklists are essential tools for ensuring consistency in PDCA implementation. For the "Plan" phase, a standardized template should be created to document goals, action plans, and metrics. Similarly, checklists can guide teams through each phase, making it easy to follow and track progress. Templates for reporting and task checklists promote efficiency and reduce the chances of overlooking key steps, supporting uniformity across departments.

Provide Training and Support for Employees

Training programs are vital for ensuring that employees understand the standardized PDCA processes. Training sessions can be organized to familiarize teams with the SOPs, templates, and checklists. Workshops and direct practice sessions can help reinforce the procedures and address questions. Ongoing support should be available to employees as they apply PDCA to various projects. This support fosters confidence in using standardized processes and reinforces the value of consistency.

Monitor Adherence to Standard Processes

Adherence to standardized processes should be monitored regularly to ensure PDCA consistency across the organization. Progress should be tracked, and compliance with SOPs and templates should be checked during reviews. When deviations occur, they should be addressed through corrective action, and any necessary adjustments to the standardized procedures should be made. Monitoring helps maintain a high standard of process consistency, reinforcing the importance of adhering to the established PDCA approach.

Facilitate Continuous Improvement in Standardized Processes

Continuous improvement should be encouraged even in a standardized system. Employees should provide feedback on the effectiveness of SOPs, templates, and checklists.

Adjustments should be made if certain aspects of the standardized processes need refinement or updates. By maintaining a flexible approach to standardization, the organization can keep its processes relevant and effective as needs change.

Foster a Culture of Consistency and Accountability

A culture of accountability is necessary for PDCA to be consistently applied across all levels. Leadership should set an example by adhering to standardized processes, and teams should be encouraged to follow these guidelines responsibly. Recognizing and rewarding teams for maintaining consistency reinforces the prizing of standardized PDCA application. This culture of accountability ensures that each team member understands their role in systematically applying the PDCA cycle.

Standardizing PDCA processes helps ensure teams across an organization follow a uniform approach, leading to more consistent outcomes and smoother collaboration. By establishing clear guidelines, providing training, and implementing tools like SOPs, templates, and checklists, PDCA can be applied at every level. When these elements are monitored, adjusted as needed, and supported by a culture of accountability, the organization can maximize the benefits of PDCA, achieving steady improvements at scale.

Leveraging Technology to Support PDCA

PDCA for Ongoing Success emphasizes how technology can enhance the effectiveness of the PDCA cycle by supporting automation, tracking, and optimization. Leveraging digital tools allows teams to focus on high-impact activities, reduces manual efforts, and improves the consistency of PDCA applications across an organization. Below, I summarize how various tools can be used in each phase of the PDCA cycle, along with their practical applications.

1. Plan Phase—Tools for Goal Setting and Data Collection

The *Plan* phase is where objectives are defined, problems are identified, and data is gathered to plan a detailed action plan. Technology tools help streamline these tasks and ensure all information is easily accessible.

- **Project Management Software (Microsoft Project, Trello, Asana)**: These tools define project goals, create timelines, and assign tasks. Teams can use boards, lists, and cards to organize steps within the PDCA cycle, making planning activities and setting milestones easy.
- **Data Collection Tools (Google Forms, SurveyMonkey)**: Data collection software helps gather feedback or survey data needed for problem analysis. These tools can compile structured data from employees, customers, or stakeholders.
- **Analytical Tools (Microsoft Excel, Tableau)**: Data analysis software analyzes historical performance data. Spreadsheets and visualization tools can perform trend analyses, identify root causes, and set measurable goals.

2. Do Phase—Tools for Task Execution and Collaboration

The *Do* phase focuses on executing the planned actions. Digital collaboration tools ensure all team members stay connected, enabling real-time communication and task management.

- **Task Management Software (Microsoft Planner, Monday.com, ClickUp)**: Task management platforms help assign and track tasks, ensuring every team member knows their responsibilities and deadlines. This allows

teams to monitor progress in real time, promoting accountability and transparency.
- **Communication Platforms (Google Meet, Microsoft Teams, Zoom)**: These platforms facilitate quick updates, discussions, and problem-solving. These tools allow teams to exchange updates, address challenges, and collaborate effectively, even remotely.
- **Workflow Automation Tools (Zapier, Microsoft Power Automate)**: These tools help automate repetitive tasks. For example, Zapier can automate notifications, report generation, and reminders, helping the team focus on core tasks without manual follow-up.

3. Check Phase–Tools for Monitoring and Evaluation

In the *Check* phase, results are reviewed against established objectives. Technology tools enable teams to track progress, evaluate performance, and detect areas needing improvement.

- **Data Visualization Software (Power BI, Google Data Studio)**: These platforms enable teams to create dashboards and reports to track KPIs in real time. Power BI, for instance, can monitor project metrics, identify trends, and share insights.
- **Quality Management Software (Qualtrax, Master control)**: Quality management tools support evaluation by recording and analyzing quality metrics. These tools monitor quality standards, document compliance, and gather information for corrective actions.
- **Feedback Tools (Google Forms, Microsoft Forms)**: Feedback tools collect input from team members, customers, or stakeholders. For instance, feedback can gather insights into customer satisfaction.

4. Act Phase—Tools for Continuous Improvement and Adjustments

The *Act* phase focuses on implementing improvements based on insights gained during the *Check* phase. Technology helps document changes, communicate lessons learned, and ensure continuous improvement.

- ➢ **Knowledge Management Systems (Confluence, Google Drive)**: Knowledge management platforms document lessons learned and standardize processes. Confluence, for example, enables teams to create a repository of best practices, making it easier for other teams to replicate success.
- ➢ **Performance Tracking Software (Tableau, Power BI)**: Performance-tracking platforms enable teams to monitor the outcomes of implemented changes. These tools ensure the new processes deliver the intended results, with ongoing tracking to ensure sustainability.

Practical Application of Digital Tools in the PDCA Cycle

Integrating these tools into PDCA can transform teams' operations and productivity, empowering them with control. For example, project management software sets up timelines in the Plan phase, while data collection tools capture relevant insights. During the *Do* phase, task management software assigns specific responsibilities, ensuring each team member understands their role. As part of the *Check* phase, data visualization software tracks KPIs in real time, enabling adjustments when results deviate from targets. In the *Act* phase, knowledge management systems help document improvements for future reference, and performance-tracking software evaluates results over the long term.

Technology tools provide the structure, clarity, and automation necessary to make PDCA scalable across teams and departments.

Using these tools at each phase makes the PDCA cycle more efficient, reliable, and adaptable. With the right digital solutions, organizations can enhance collaboration, ensure consistency, and maintain a continuous improvement culture at scale.

Training Teams for Scalable Implementation

Managers and team leaders are responsible for training teams for scalable implementation. It is essential to ensure that the PDCA (Plan-Do-Check-Act) methodology becomes an integral part of the organization's culture and is effectively applied by employees at all levels. When employees understand and consistently practice PDCA, small-scale improvements can be extended across the organization, promoting a continuous improvement mindset. This approach requires a structured training strategy focused on clarity, consistency, and support to empower teams.

To begin with, a foundational understanding of PDCA principles should be provided to all team members. Basic training can be delivered through workshops or online modules, focusing on each stage of the PDCA cycle—planning, implementing, checking results, and making adjustments. By breaking down the cycle into these four stages, employees are introduced to a clear framework that simplifies problem-solving and encourages systematic improvements. Case studies can show how PDCA has been successfully applied in similar contexts, and practical, relatable training.

Once the fundamentals of PDCA are covered, it's crucial to encourage hands-on practice to solidify the concepts. This phase involves applying PDCA on small projects or existing processes, allowing employees to experience the cycle firsthand. By working on actual issues and projects within the organization, they can see the impact of PDCA on improving outcomes and solving problems efficiently. During this stage, team members are encouraged to ask questions and seek guidance, ensuring that any uncertainties are addressed early in the learning process. This hands-on practice is a key component of PDCA training, as it reinforces the learning and helps employees understand the practical application of the methodology.

In addition, resources such as PDCA toolkits or templates should be made available to help guide employees through each stage. These materials can include checklists, process maps, and flowcharts that simplify the application of PDCA and provide a structured approach to each task. Visual aids also help ensure that each stage is addressed systematically, reducing the risk of skipping steps or overlooking key actions. Employees will feel more confident and empowered when they have easy-to-use tools that help them understand and apply the PDCA cycle.

Regular feedback and progress reviews reinforce learning and refining skills, making the audience feel more involved and accountable. Managers and team leaders can facilitate this by setting aside time for review sessions where teams share their PDCA experiences, discuss challenges, and highlight successful applications. Constructive feedback can be provided during these sessions, focusing on areas that need improvement or reinforcement. By having open discussions about the PDCA process, team members become more comfortable adapting the methodology and refining their approaches.

Mentorship and support from experienced PDCA practitioners are valuable, providing a safety net for less experienced team members. Assigning mentors or PDCA champions within the organization allows them to learn from those who have successfully applied the method. Mentorship helps ensure PDCA practices are consistently upheld by providing insights, practical advice, and encouragement. This approach creates a support network that fosters a collaborative environment where employees feel encouraged to apply PDCA.

Progress tracking systems can be implemented to measure the effectiveness of PDCA training. This can involve monitoring key performance indicators (KPIs) that reflect improvements made through PDCA, such as reductions in process times, cost savings, or increases in efficiency. By reviewing these metrics, the organization can assess the impact of PDCA training on overall performance and identify any areas that may need further reinforcement.

Last, continuous reinforcement of PDCA training through refresher courses or advanced sessions is recommended. More complex training on advanced techniques can be introduced as teams become proficient in the basic PDCA cycle. This ensures that employees remain engaged and continue to deepen their understanding, allowing PDCA to develop alongside the organization's needs.

With consistent and structured training, employees at all levels will be equipped to apply PDCA effectively. This approach will foster a culture of continuous improvement, enabling scalable PDCA implementation as a sustainable, impactful growth strategy across the organization.

Monitoring Long-Term Growth and Success

Monitoring long-term growth and success is essential for sustaining the impact of PDCA (Plan-Do-Check-Act). When efforts are consistently measured and analyzed, the benefits of continuous improvement can be realized across the organization. The effectiveness of PDCA depends not only on short-term wins but also on the ability to achieve sustainable growth that aligns with strategic goals. Long-term growth measurement can help identify trends, improve processes, and adapt strategies for ongoing success.

Key performance indicators (KPIs) play a crucial role in evaluating the long-term impact of the PDCA cycle. Choosing KPIs based on the organization's priorities, such as quality improvements, cost reductions, customer satisfaction, or employee engagement, can help form a clear picture of progress. These indicators should be monitored consistently to ensure that the goals set in the PDCA planning phase are met and that improvements are sustained.

Once KPIs are established, regular data collection should be conducted to track progress. Data should be gathered periodically to capture performance changes and analyze patterns. By maintaining accurate, up-to-date records, teams can assess the impact of improvements, detect issues, and prevent recurring challenges. Automation tools, where possible, can streamline data collection and ensure accuracy, minimizing the time spent on manual tracking.

Ongoing trend analysis is vital to understanding the actual impact of PDCA on long-term growth. Positive and negative patterns can reveal whether implemented changes achieve the desired outcomes. For instance, if a process improvement shows positive results initially but performance declines later, further investigation can help identify the reasons behind the decline. This understanding allows corrective actions to be taken, ensuring that improvements continue supporting long-term growth.

Adjustments should be made based on the insights gained from monitoring. PDCA encourages adaptation, and strategy changes should be made whenever necessary to keep the organization aligned with growth objectives. Regular PDCA cycles should assess whether current strategies remain effective. Suppose the analysis reveals that goals must be met or results will stagnate. In that case, reviewing the planning stage may be necessary to redefine objectives or identify new improvement opportunities.

This adaptability helps keep the organization responsive and proactive in its growth approach.

Feedback from stakeholders, including employees, customers, and partners, should be integrated into long-term monitoring. Gathering feedback can provide insights into customer satisfaction and employee engagement, which are critical to evaluating the impact of PDCA. Feedback also offers an external perspective, highlighting aspects that data alone may not capture. Regular feedback loops foster continuous improvement, enabling the organization to better align its practices with the needs and expectations of its stakeholders.

Progress reviews should be conducted with teams responsible for PDCA implementation to ensure accountability. These reviews discuss progress toward long-term goals, and any required adjustments can be planned. Performance reports summarizing growth metrics and highlighting key achievements can be shared with leadership to ensure alignment with the organization's strategic vision.

A commitment to learning and adapting based on long-term monitoring results should be encouraged. Teams should be motivated to reflect on outcomes, celebrate successes, and acknowledge areas for further improvement. This focus on continuous improvement ensures that PDCA becomes part of the organizational culture and that growth remains consistent.

In summary, monitoring long-term growth and success through PDCA provides a roadmap for sustained improvement. By measuring, analyzing, and adapting, an organization can maintain momentum, respond to challenges, and lay a foundation for ongoing progress aligned with its goals.

Summary of Chapter 8: *Scaling PDCA for Growth*

Once PDCA has been adopted within teams and departments, the next step is to scale these practices across the organization. This chapter provides a roadmap for expanding PDCA beyond small-scale improvements to a broader organizational level. Strategies for standardizing processes and creating consistency in PDCA applications are discussed, along with the role of technology in tracking and optimizing PDCA activities. By implementing tools and software, organizations can enhance visibility into performance and streamline the cycle for larger-scale operations. Tips for training employees and fostering a culture of continuous improvement at every level of the organization are included to support sustained growth.

****

Book Summary of PDCA For Ongoing Success

The PDCA for Ongoing Success book explores the transformative power of the PDCA cycle—Plan, Do, Check, Act—as a structured, iterative approach to continuous improvement. This method allows businesses and teams to improve processes, solve problems, and drive sustainable growth. The book provides a comprehensive guide on using PDCA to foster operational efficiency, enhance decision-making, and create a culture of ongoing progress. It focuses on practical implementation strategies, real-world case studies, and critical insights to ensure that each stage of the PDCA cycle delivers measurable results.

Chapter 1: Introduction

In the opening chapter, readers are introduced to the foundations of PDCA, including its history, principles, and core benefits. PDCA originated as a method to enhance quality and problem-solving in manufacturing, but it has since evolved into a versatile framework across industries and organizational functions. The cycle starts with the *Plan* phase, where objectives are set, potential solutions are explored, and a roadmap for action is created. The *Do* phase involves executing the plan and observing the results. In the *Check* phase, data is analyzed to assess whether the objectives were met. In the Act phase, adjustments are made to refine processes and prepare for the next cycle.

Chapter 2: Planning for Problem-Solving

Planning is the cornerstone of successful PDCA implementation. This chapter details the importance of clear, measurable goal setting to guide problem-solving efforts. Specific goal-setting tools, such as SMART objectives, are explained to help create effective plans. This phase also involves identifying resources and responsibilities, developing actionable steps, and assessing risks to prepare for potential obstacles. Planning is a systematic process that lays the foundation for effective execution and reliable outcomes.

Chapter 3: Effective Execution in the Do Phase

Execution is critical for turning plans into actions. The *Do* phase focuses on implementing the strategies outlined in the *Plan* phase, ensuring that each task aligns with the established goals. This chapter offers guidance on breaking down complex solutions into manageable tasks, assigning responsibilities, and setting timelines to keep the team on track. Real-time monitoring is emphasized to allow adjustments, enabling teams to respond quickly to unforeseen issues. Practical tips for maintaining team alignment and accountability during execution are provided to streamline the process.

Chapter 4: Measuring Performance

The *Check* phase evaluates results against the goals set in the planning stage. This chapter highlights how to define key performance indicators (KPIs) and collect accurate data to gauge success. Various data collection techniques are explored to ensure reliable measurements, and tools for real-time monitoring are discussed to enable responsive adjustments. By analyzing outcomes, organizations can determine the effectiveness of their strategies, identify gaps, and recognize opportunities for improvement. This phase reinforces the PDCA cycle's emphasis on learning from results and making data-driven decisions.

Chapter 5: Learning and Adapting

The *Act* phase of the PDCA cycle is where continuous improvement takes shape. This chapter explores how insights gained from the *Check* phase can refine strategies and adapt plans for the next cycle. By closing the feedback loop, organizations can enhance their processes, reduce waste, and drive growth. Strategies for applying lessons learned and techniques for fostering a culture of continuous learning and adaptation are provided. This chapter emphasizes the importance of prizing reflection and feedback as essential components of long-term success.

Chapter 6: Applying PDCA in Teams

Aligning teams around PDCA is essential for effective implementation. This chapter outlines how team members can collaborate to refine processes, solve problems, and achieve shared goals. Prizing clarity of roles is emphasized, ensuring each team member understands their responsibilities within the PDCA cycle. Techniques for fostering open communication and accountability are provided, along with strategies for celebrating achievements and learning from experiences together. The chapter encourages a collaborative mindset, strengthening teams' commitment to continuous improvement.

Chapter 7: Case Studies in PDCA

Real-world case studies illustrate the practical impact of PDCA across industries. Each case study examines how a leading company successfully applied PDCA to address challenges, improve efficiency, and achieve strategic objectives. For example, Toyota's pioneering use of PDCA to enhance manufacturing efficiency is explored, showing how the cycle contributed to the company's lean manufacturing success. Other cases, such as Amazon's customer satisfaction initiatives and Intel's product development process optimization, demonstrate how PDCA can drive innovation and deliver results across different organizational functions. Each example serves as a roadmap for readers to understand how to apply PDCA effectively.

Chapter 8: Scaling PDCA for Growth

Once PDCA has been adopted within teams and departments, the next step is to scale these practices across the organization. This chapter provides a roadmap for expanding PDCA beyond small-scale improvements to a broader organizational level. Strategies for standardizing processes and creating consistency in PDCA applications are discussed, along with the role of technology in tracking and optimizing PDCA activities. By implementing tools and software, organizations can enhance visibility into performance and streamline the cycle for larger-scale operations. Tips for training employees and fostering a culture of continuous improvement at every level of the organization are included to support sustained growth.

Conclusion: PDCA as a Tool for Ongoing Success

The book concludes by reinforcing the value of PDCA as a tool for achieving ongoing success. It emphasizes that PDCA is not a one-time approach but a cycle that thrives on repetition and refinement. The iterative nature of PDCA enables organizations to keep growing, making them resilient and adaptable in the face of change. Readers are encouraged to view PDCA as a mindset as much as a process, embedding its principles in their daily work to foster continuous improvement. By following the PDCA guidance *for Ongoing Success*, individuals and organizations can unlock the potential for lasting growth and operational excellence.

This book shows readers how to use the PDCA process through real-life examples and actionable steps, providing the tools for continued improvement. Whether applied to small projects or organization-wide initiatives, PDCA is presented as a transformative approach to mastering the art of improvement.

A Heartfelt Request

Thank you for choosing *PDCA for Ongoing Success*. With so many books out there, I'm genuinely honored that you selected mine. I hope the insights and strategies have added value to your journey toward continuous improvement and success.

Now, **may I ask for a small favor?** It will take just 30 seconds of your time, but it would mean the world to me. Could you leave a review for the book?

https://www.amazon.com/PDCA-Ongoing-Success-Decision-Making-Sustainable-ebook/dp/B0DPSK5YQJ/

For independent authors like me, reviews are everything. They help new readers discover the book and encourage them to take a chance on its message. Your feedback can make a big difference in helping this book reach others who might benefit from it.

Writing a review is quick and simple. Click the link below to take you to the book's review page. Even a few words can make a lasting impact.

Your support is invaluable, and I'm deeply grateful for your time and encouragement. Thank you for helping me share this work with a broader audience. I can't wait to hear your thoughts!

Free Bonus- Audiobook

Experience *PDCA for Ongoing Success* for Free on YouTube

Unlock the secrets of continuous improvement with the **free audiobook version** of *PDCA for Ongoing Success*. This transformative guide takes you through the PDCA (Plan-Do-Check-Act) cycle principles and the innovative SMART PDCA-SDCA framework, offering a proven path to efficiency, growth, and sustainable success.

Designed for business leaders, professionals, and learners alike, the audiobook offers an immersive experience that blends practical insights with real-world examples from global giants such as Toyota, Amazon, and Netflix. Whether you're seeking to streamline processes, improve decision-making, or cultivate a culture of adaptability, this audiobook is your trusted companion.

Why listen for free? **Growth should be accessible.** This YouTube audiobook lets you learn on the go—during your commute, workout, or downtime. The engaging narration ensures clarity, while the structured chapters offer actionable steps to drive immediate impact in your organization.

Click the link, immerse yourself in the wisdom of continuous improvement, and share the journey with your team. Let this audiobook inspire new possibilities for you and your organization. Your path to ongoing success starts here.

Audiobook Page link—PDCA for Ongoing Success.

Copyright © 2024

All rights reserved. This publication's content and design are protected under applicable copyright laws. No part of this book may be copied, reproduced, distributed, or transmitted in any form or by any means, whether electronic, mechanical, photocopying, recording, or otherwise, without prior written permission from the author or the publisher, **Mastermind Career Hub**.

This restriction applies to the use of this book for any purpose, including but not limited to:

1. Reproduction for commercial, educational, or private purposes.
2. Storage or retrieval through electronic systems, including data storage devices, websites, and email communication.
3. Transmission via digital platforms, including social media, websites, or online or offline distribution networks.

Exceptions to this restriction may apply in cases allowed under applicable copyright law, such as fair use for educational or critical purposes, provided that proper attribution is given. For permissions and licensing requests, please get in touch with the publisher or author in writing at
connect@mastermindcareerhub.com

Unauthorized use, duplication, or distribution of any part of this publication may cause civil and criminal penalties under copyright law.

References

1. Moen R., and Norman C., "The History of the PDCA Cycle." In Proceedings of the 7th ANQ Congress, Tokyo 2009, September 17, 2009.
2. Imai, M. 1886. Kaizen: The Key to Japan's Competitive Success. New York: Random House.
3. [17] Langley, G., Nolan, K, and Nolan, T. 1994. The Foundation of Improvement, Quality Progress, June 1994.
4. The Improvement Guide: A Practical Approach to Enhancing Organizational Performance By Gerald J. Langley, Ronald D. Moen, Kevin M. Nolan, Thomas W. Nolan, Clifford L. Norman, Lloyd P. Provost · 2009.
5. Jain R.K. and Trivedi H. M., "Quality Management for Zero Defect and Zero Effect." ASQ India, 2018.
6. Manos A. And Vincent C., The LEAN Handbook, ASQ Quality Press, 2013.
7. ASQ-LED-Webinar-2-2021-Turning-the-SDCA-Cycle-for-Daily-Management-Watson
   https://www.youtube.com/watch?v=WcVYbUH1T0U
8. https://deming.org/explore/pdsa/
9. https://www.qualityze.com/blogs/pdca-cycle-for-continuous-improvement-in-organizations
10. https://asq.org/quality-resources/pdca-cycle
11. https://www.performancemagazine.org/pdca-pdsa-philosophy-performance/
12. https://www.lean.org/lexicon-terms/pdca/
13. https://www.nature.com/articles/s41598-023-42295-8
14. https://asana.com/resources/pdca-cycle
15. https://whatfix.com/blog/pdca-cycle/
16. https://www.researchgate.net/publication/343384691_Plan_do_check_action_PDCA_method_literature_review_and_research_issues
17. https://en.wikipedia.org/wiki/PDCA
18. https://www.techtarget.com/whatis/definition/PDCA-plan-do-check-act
19. https://www.mindtools.com/as2l5i1/pdca-plan-do-check-act
20. https://www.investopedia.com/terms/p/pdca-cycle.asp
21. https://www.researchgate.net/publication/377046658_Benefits_using_PDCA_cycle_of_continuous_improvement_in_manufacturing_industry_-_a_case_study/link/66064f8cb839e05a20a8d5f2/download?_tp=eyJjb250ZXh0Ijp7ImZpcnN0UGFnZSI6InB1YmxpY2F0aW9uIiwicGFnZSI6InB1YmxpY2F0aW9uIn19

www.ingramcontent.com/pod-product-compliance
Lightning Source LLC
Chambersburg PA
CBHW071548220526
45469CB00003B/945